THE SUCCESS FACTOR

THE
SUCCESS
FACTOR

SUCCEEDING IN BUSINESS AND IN LIFE

H.E. STANTON

An OPTIMA book

First published in Australia in 1988 by
William Collins Pty Ltd
This edition first published in the UK in 1988 by
Macdonald Optima, a division of
Macdonald & Co. (Publishers) Ltd

A member of Maxwell Pergamon Publishing Corporation plc

British Library Cataloguing in Publication Data

Stanton, H.E. (Harry E.)
Success factor.
    1. Personal success
    I. Title
    158'.1

    ISBN 0-356-15908-6

Macdonald & Co. (Publishers) Ltd
3rd Floor
Greater London House
Hampstead Road
London NW1 7QX

Photoset in Times Roman

Printed and bound in Great Britain by
The Guernsey Press Co. Ltd., Guernsey, Channel Islands.

Contents

1 What is Success?

DEFINING SUCCESS

Bob Hanlon is a hard-driving businessman. He works long hours, takes home a bulging brief-case every weekend and is always ready to accept extra responsibility. For behaving in this way, he is rewarded with a large salary, rapid promotion and considerable international travel. However, because his time is so committed to his work, he has little time for his family or for leisure activities. Is Bob a success?

Paul Thompson is a university lecturer. Quiet and unambitious, Paul has, for many years, occupied the same position, one in which he seems likely to remain for the foreseeable future. He is an excellent teacher, produces competent research publications and serves on a number of committees. He does relatively little university work at home, preferring to spend a lot of time with his family and on his hobby of woodworking. Is Paul a success?

Maureen Bishop is a housewife. She has raised three children, as well as providing great support for her businessman husband, entertaining his clients and ensuring home problems do not interfere with his work. With a wide range of interests embracing art, craftwork and music, Maureen enjoys an active social life with many friends. Is Maureen a success?

Attempting to place a valuation on the success or otherwise of someone's life is a rather hazardous endeavour. This is because we are prone to impose our own definitions on someone else who does not, perhaps, share our values. We all believe we are normal and that our way of thinking is shared by the rest of the world.

In America, the dollar has been generally accepted as the measure of success. The more money a person has, the more successful he or she is assumed to be. In his book *Success*, Michael Korda suggests that we should never forget that:

> Money comes first . . . greed pays off. If you're any good at all, you're probably worth more than you are asking . . . the purpose of business is to produce profit, so don't be ashamed of making a profit for yourself.

However, not all cultures accept this measure. Nor do all Americans see money as *the* index of success. It is really a matter of goals, for they enshrine what we perceive as important. For some of us, having lots of money is vital. For others, having considerable leisure time to spend as we wish is of prime importance. It usually comes down to achieving a balance between work, family life and leisure activities so that a sense of contentment is attained.

One rather cynical view of success can be found in *Ginger, You're Barmy*, David Lodge's devastating critique of the army as seen through the eyes of a young man doing National Service in England. In an adverse situation, his goal was to make life as pleasant for himself as possible.

> All human activity was useless, but some kinds were more pleasant than others. . . . There was no such thing as society: just a collection of little self-contained boxes, roped untidily together and set adrift to float aimlessly on the waters of time, the occupants of each box convinced that theirs was the most important box, heedless of the claims of the rest. Success did not consist in getting into the box where most power was exercised: there were many people who were powerful and unhappy. Success consisted in determining which box would be most pleasant for you, and getting into it.

Each of the three people described at the beginning of this chapter has a goal. The extent to which they achieve these can be a way of defining their success. If Bob's goal is making a lot of money, he is successful. Paul is not wealthy nor is he likely to become so, yet we would not dub him unsuccessful because of this. Money in of no great significance to him. The enjoyment of his family and his hobby is far more important, and, if he is able to create time to achieve this goal, he too may be seen as successful.

In the eyes of many, Maureen would not be perceived as a success. She could be seen as living her life in a subsidary role, supporting a husband who actually does things while she stays home with the children. Yet Maureen may have derived tremendous satisfaction from her role as a mother and wife, feeling a sense of personal worth as she revels in the warmth of the family life she has created. If she does experience this satisfaction, it would seem that she, too, is a success.

THE IMPORTANCE OF GOALS

To engender a sense of fulfilment, goals do not have to be grandiose. To begin with a reasonably realistic aim and achieve it is eminently preferable to striving for something so far beyond your reach that you are bound to fail. Establishing realistic aims creates the habit of succeeding. Each day you can set up goals, no matter how small, and as you attain them you can gradually raise your sights until your achievements become greater.

It has been said that happiness is not a station you arrive at, but a manner of travelling. Similarily, it is helpful to think of success as a journey rather than as a specific destination. During the course of that journey, your goals may undergo frequent changes, your ambitions may enlarge or contract. To focus too intently upon a destination, no matter how appealing, is likely to be unrewarding. Many people find that when they have achieved 'the attributes of success', such as a good home, plenty of money, prestige, they feel unfulfilled, empty, and the sense of 'Is that all there is?' is strong within them.

With changing goals and an interesting journey, we can experience success over and over again. This is likely to be beneficial. Anatole de Laforge put it well when he said: 'All the virtues and all the joys of living are contained in one word—success.'

Somerset Maugham made the same point in a somewhat different way:

> The common idea that success spoils people by making them vain, egotistic, and self-complacent is erroneous; on the contrary it makes them, for the most part, humble, tolerant, and kind. Failure makes people bitter and cruel.

As Maugham says, we do have erroneous ideas about success. Convention has it that the successful businessman invariably pays the price in hypertension, heart attacks, ulcers, impotence and other stress-related illness. The truth is somewhat different. Successful executives, according to United States insurance figures, tend to enjoy a longer life and better health than the average American.

Because there seems to be great physical and mental benefit in mobilising all our resources to achieve success, Michael Korda, the author of *Success*, suggests that failure may be one of the least recognised health hazards. He quotes the case of a colleague, stagnant in his job, who suffered very badly from asthma. This man, against the advice of friends who felt his health would break under the strain, took on a new challenge, a different job with exciting responsibilities. Far from succcumbing to stress, this man's health improved dramatically, his asthma disappearing entirely.

Cases such as this suggest that because inertia is a way of refusing challenge and change, it often creates physical symptoms, such as asthma. Thus we underachieve. Yet, when the stimulus of a new job or a new environment is accepted, our bodies tend to respond very positively, throwing off the previously disabling 'illness'. Meeting the new challenge, feeling the success of achievement, seems to give us a new lease of life. We feel we are using our potential to virtually reshape our lives.

THE FEAR OF SUCCESS

Success seems to be a revitalizing life force whereas failure exerts a deadening effect. The latter tends to sour our lives, to make them far less enjoyable than they could otherwise be. Yet, strangely enough, we may actually be frightened of success. Many and varied are the ways in which we cause ourselves to fail, so devious in fact that we may remain quite unaware that we are sabotaging ourselves.

Notice how often we choose the wrong jobs, stay in relationships which are destructive, behave in ways which ensure we will not achieve the goals we seek, emphasize our weaknesses rather than our strengths, and programme ourselves negatively to expect failure rather than positively to expect success.

Possibly the most all-pervading way we show our fear of success is by staying put, accepting something less than we really want, rather than taking action. Instead of doing something positive, we make all sorts of rationalizations about why things have to stay as they are. Sure, success implies risks, and it is reasonable to evaluate these by identifying those which are rational from those which are irrational. Weighing up the advantages and disadvantages of seeking a particular promotion is rational: feeling that there is no point in applying because 'things never work out well for me' is irrational. This is destructive because a self-fulfilling prophecy ensuring future failure is created.

Success is more pleasant than failure. Though it may not eliminate all life's major traumas, the old song puts it well with the line: 'It's better being miserable with than without'. Most of us want to succeed, yet many of us are held back by the self-engendered fear that we are not good enough. Sometimes we may be right. More often we are wrong. We sell ourselves short. So, instead of fearing success, embrace the factors which contribute to goal achievement. Though it has been said that **desire, determination and a good sense of timing are the key elements in success**, other factors make a contribution too.

ACCEPTING RESPONSIBILITY

Some qualities, such as loyalty, can be faked. As long as you publicly display loyalty to both subordinates and superiors, you gain respect, even if covertly you are working against them to ensure your own advancement.

However, this form of deceit is really not possible with responsibility where, to be successful, you must be willing to accept personal accountability in the meeting of precisely specified goals. You must also accept personal responsibility for the behaviour of those who work for you.

Many of us fear to take responsibility because of self-doubt. As Alexandre Dumas put it: 'The man who doubts himself is like the soldier who enlists in the ranks of his enemies and bears arms against himself'. In other words, we use hypnosis, which is primarily a powerful form of suggestion, to convince ourselves that we are not worthy.

However, if we are good at practising this negative form of self-hypnosis, it is likely that we are equally adept at using positive self-hypnosis. The same process is involved: simply that of feeding ourselves suggestions. The only difference is that we use positives instead of negatives.

Become aware of what you are suggesting to yourself by tuning into your inner dialogue from time to time. You are constantly talking to yourself, sometimes out loud, sometimes silently. Much of what you tell yourself is appalling for it can so often be a stream of blame, condemnation, criticism, and self-destruction. You wouldn't talk to a friend that way, so why talk to yourself in such negatives ways?

Overcome this tendency by playing a game with yourself. Each day make it a challenge to become aware of the 'downputting' comments you subject yourself to and to deliberately change them into their opposites. You don't have to believe these opposites. Just make the changes. What you are doing is feeding a different programme into your unconscious, a part of your mind which you can regard as acting much like a computer. If you consistently change your negative messages into positive ones, self-doubt will become become transformed into self-confidence.

To reach out and accept new responsibilies requires a belief in your own self-worth. By this I do not mean that you have to feel superior to other people. It is not so much a matter of comparing yourself with others. Rather, it is simply a respect for your own worth and value as a human being, for your own strengths, special abilities and competence.

Fear of others does not usually hold you back from assuming additional responsibilities. More commonly it is fear of yourself, a lack of faith in yourself. As you take on more responsibility, this will provide the opportunity for you to grow. Certainly risks are involved, yet if you want to be successful, there is simply no way you can achieve this without being prepared to take some chances. In fact, many very successful people have found that the quickest way of getting ahead is to deliberately seek out the high risk tasks. They do this in a realistic way, however, for realism is another factor which makes an important contribution to success.

REALISM

Ray Harvey is a manipulator. He is able to persuade people to buy insurance cover they may not really need. His record indicates that he is very successful, a success based primarily on his ability to see things realistically. Thus he has a relatively clear concept of how the world actually works. Competitors say that Ray is positively Machiavellian, this being a reference to the sixteenth-century philosopher-statesman who had the temerity to set down on paper the cold-blooded realities of assuming and keeping power.

According to Machiavelli, if we are to be successful we must be able to detach ourselves from those with whom we deal, not allowing ourselves to become emotionally involved. Free from the fatal error of permitting emotions to affect judgement, we can make decisions coolly and realistically.

To Machiavelli, being realistic meant seeing men as they are:

> . . . ungrateful, fickle, false, cowardly, covetous, and as long as you succeed, they are yours entirely: they will offer you their blood, property, life and children when the need is far distant; but when it approaches they turn against you.

Accordingly, people who rate high in their possession of the Machiavellian characteristic do not have a particularly high opinion of their fellow man. For this, they come in for a lot of criticism. Yet anyone who has much experience of the cut-throat environment that is the business world would probably agree that such an opinion is more realistic than one which emphasizes man's inherent goodness.

In Ray's field, for example, salesmen of policies usually strive to sell more insurance than is actually wanted because it is in their pecuniary interest to do so. Similarily, most advertising exhorts us to buy products which we do not need and which rarely live up to the claims made for them.

Business involves competition, antagonism, deceit and many other elements which we would prefer did not exist. But they do exist, and the Machiavellian person recognizes this. His coolness and detachment enable him to deal successfully with others because his expectations are low. He subscribes to Murphy's Law, recognizing that things which can go wrong will go wrong and that 'If everything seems to be going well, you don't know what the hell is going on'.

Ray's realism shows itself in his attitude of never taking it for granted that people will do what they have been told to do, or that they will act in ways which are rational and reasonable. He assumes that errors and delays are a part of life, though he attempts to minimize these by close supervision of his staff. He would like the salesmen who work for him to show the same dedication and application that he does, but he knows this is unlikely to happen. In short, like most successful people, Ray does not so much manipulate as allow for error and irrationality in the people with whom he deals.

This ability to view the world in a detached, unemotional way, which has been termed the Machiavellian factor, is, like other personality characteristics, present in us all to a greater or lesser extent. By using the pencil and paper test outlined on page 18, it is possible to gain a rough idea of how Machiavellian you are. However, the score which you derive from this test is only an indication of the degree to which you believe that people in general can be manipulated. It does not necessarily mean that you would, or do, manipulate other people.

To get some idea of whether you rate as a high or a low Machiavellian, check the point on the scale that most closely represents your attitude. To find your Mach score, add the numbers you have checked on questions 1, 3, 4, 5, 9 and 10. For the other four questions, reverse the numbers you checked—5 becomes 1, 4 is 2, 1 is 5. Total your 10 numbers. This is your score. A survey conducted in American found that their national average was 25.

High Machiavellians tend to be pragmatic, accepting things as they are. Low Machiavellians are more inclined to see things as they want them to be, or wish they were, and to act as if that is how they really are. Naturally

A test

Are you Machiavellian?

	Disagree			Agree	
	a lot	a little	neutral	a little	a lot
1 The best way to handle people is to tell them what they want to hear.	1	2	3	4	5
2 When you ask someone to do something for you, it is best to give the real reasons for wanting it rather than giving reasons which might carry more weight.	1	2	3	4	5
3 Anyone who completely trusts anyone else is asking for trouble.	1	2	3	4	5
4 It is hard to get ahead without cutting corners here and there.	1	2	3	4	5
5 It is safest to asume that all people have a vicious streak and it will come out when they are given a chance.	1	2	3	4	5
6 One should take action only when sure it is morally right.	1	2	3	4	5
7 Most people are basically good and kind.	1	2	3	4	5
8 There is no excuse for lying to someone else.	1	2	3	4	5
9 Most men forget more easily the death of their father than the loss of their property.	1	2	3	4	5
10 Generally speaking, men won't work hard unless they're forced to do so.	1	2	3	4	5

enough, they often get their fingers burned. On the other hand, it is possible to be too cynical, anticipating nothing but trouble from others, and getting what we expect. As in most things, moderation produces better results than extremism.

It is primarily from our own experience that we become realistic. Everyone makes mistakes, even the most successful amongst us. However, success is often a function of how well we learn from these mistakes so that we do not repeat the errors of the past.

Not that we are likely to achieve perfection. To expect to do so is unrealistic, given the imperfect character of human beings, and is a sure way to create an unhappy life. Perfectionists are doomed to failure, for they set goals which are unattainable. No matter how well they perform, perfection will elude them, thus disappointment and frustration are constant companions. This fact of life should be stored away carefully in our memories.

MEMORY

Possession of a good memory is another factor which contributes to success. We can all have good memories if we exert a little effort, for remembering something is primarily a matter of concentrating upon it when first it comes to our attention. For us to make this effort of concentration, we have to want to remember that particular thing. It must matter to us, we have to care about it enough to try to remember it. Unless we do make this effort, attempting to recall it at a later date is likely to be unsuccessful.

I still recollect, with admiration, how Richard, the newly-appointed Vice-Chancellor of a university where I was teaching, called most of the academics, office staff, gardeners and maintenance staff by their names within the first month of his taking up office. He felt it was essential to do this, for it demonstrated his belief that the staff mattered, that they were sufficiently important for him to learn their names as quickly as possible. A very sensible man, for it has been said that the sound of our own name is the most important sound in the English language. By using peoples' names, the Vice-Chancellor conferred upon them a sense of self-worth.

To learn the names quickly, Richard would take an active interest in the person to whom he was introduced, perhaps asking how the name was spelt, then write this down as soon as it was convenient to do so. He would also write down the person's job and any personal characteristic which was at all unusual.

If he had difficulty with a particular name, Richard would use mental imagery to impress it on his memory. For example, should one of the maintenance men have the name of Coldstock, he might visualize this man with a block of ice on his head within which was the stock of a rifle. This linking of names with unusual images, though sometimes criticized as useless, stood Richard in good stead. He employed it most effectively to learn names quickly. Should you wish to use this technique yourself, keep it in mind that the more bizarre the image you create, the more likely you are to recall the name you have linked to that image.

Obviously behaving like this takes time. Whether you want to spend time in this way depends on the importance you attach to remembering the names of the people with whom you come into contact. Memory is basically a matter of motivation. The person who remembers all the details of an involved business deal, but forgets the names of his wife's friends is obviously more interested in the former than the latter. This is, not uncommonly, carried to the extent where the businessman also forgets his wife's birthday and their wedding anniversary. This indicates where his interests lie and, if he wants to keep harmony in the home, he needs to develop some means of keeping track of such information.

Writing it down seems an obvious solution. We often impose a quite unnecessary burden on our minds by attempting to memorize many things which we can, quite easily, look up. I know I would be lost without the small diary I carry. In this I note the transient things I need to do each day as well as information about people with whom I am in regular contact. Attempting to memorize such information is unproductive when it is so easy to refer to a diary.

There are some people who reject such written prompts, claiming that it is only through constant use that we can improve our memories. Though there is some truth in this, there are really very few ways in which we can deliberately improve our memories except by becoming more motivated to use the facility we already have.

Gerontology specialists are discovering that the human brain remains quite plastic and, provided we remain sufficiently challenged, we are capable of learning until well into our eighties. Fortunately, despite popular belief to the contrary, this new learning can be remembered quite efficiently.

Although success in life involves many factors, including the ones discussed above, perhaps the four shown below are of prime importance.

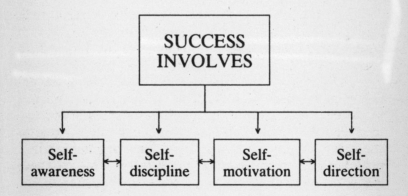

Without self-awareness, we are insensitive to our behaviour, thus we are unable to change in ways which may be of benefit to us. However, with increased awareness of our behaviour and its effects on other people, we are more likely to be able to discipline ourselves to improve these effects. Similarily, as our self-discipline grows, we can motivate ourselves more effectively to set and achieve goals we regard as important. This is self-direction, the process of establishing our own internal guidance system and using our time efficiently so we can accomplish our aims. In the following chapters each of these four shall be examined in some detail.

2 Self-Awareness

SELF-OBSERVATION

Before we can know what we are really like we need to observe ourselves in a detached way. Sometimes this happens quite spontaneously. A number of my patients have told me about their out-of-the-body experiences which felt as if they were looking down on this person, themself, still lying in bed. Because the experience frightened them, they had not talked about it to anyone else. Without exception, they were very relieved to find it was a not too uncommon occurrence, often happening when we are very tired.

Something similar occurs, too, during sport, usually when we are playing extremely well. During such a magic moment, which seems to come far too rarely, it may seem as if we are watching and marvelling at the performance of this person, ourself. We are aware both of ourself as watcher and ourself as player. A peculiar experience, but one which has been shared by many sportspeople.

In addition to these spontaneous moments, we can, if we wish, deliberately stand back and observe ourselves in action. If we did this frequently it could become somewhat tedious, but if used only from time to time, the technique is very valuable in giving us insight into how we behave.

At a dinner party, John Harrison listened to another guest rhapsodizing about the glorious sunrise he had witnessed that morning. Suitably inspired, John went to bed vowing he would get up in time to see the next morning's sunrise. Accordingly he set his alarm so it would waken him early. When the alarm sounded, John sleepily shut it off. At this time, if John had been interested in observing himself, he would have found several warring little 'I's within him. One of these was saying something like: 'I really want to see this sunrise.' However, another little 'I' might be saying: 'It is so warm and comfortable in bed, I think I'll stay here,' while yet another could speak thus: 'I wish I hadn't told everyone at the party what I intended to do. If I don't see the sunrise they'll all rubbish me.'

This concept of the little 'I's, coined by Gurdjieff, the Armenian guru, suggests that we are deluded when we act as if we are a unity comprising a single 'I'. We are not such a unity, but a mixture of warring factions which pulls us in different directions at the same time. However, once we realize this, we can identify the various little 'I's, all wanting their own way, and decide which seems best in the current situation. Because we are able to decide amongst them, this suggests there is some part of us which is uninvolved, capable of observing what is happening.

This we can refer to as soul, spirit, or, in Gurdjieff's term, essence. It is an inner 'I' which can, in a detached, objective way, watch what we do. It is as if we have this inner core, present since birth, and an outer personality which we have acquired through experience. By observing this outer personality, which is what is seen by other people, we can learn a great deal about ourselves and the way we function. This information can be put to very good use in helping us along the road to success.

Let's consider Leon Sampson, President of a Real Estate Institute ethics committee. Leon is in great demand as a speaker on the importance of sound ethical principles in all business dealings. Yet in his real estate dealings he uses every sharp practice he can to extract as much money as possible from his clients, acting quite unethically in the way he plays his clients off against one another for his own financial benefit.

Though it may appear as if Leon is a hypocrite, that is actually not the case. He is genuinely unaware that he has this great contradiction within his personality. Gurdjieff would describe him as having buffers in his mind, buffers which prevent him putting these two contradictory behaviours together and seeing their incompatibility. Leon has not cultivated the virtue of self-observation. If he had done so, not only would he have been able to do something about the contradiction referred to, but he would also have been able to detach himself from his worries.

When we worry about things we churn them over and over in our minds without getting anywhere. All we achieve when we worry is to feel bad, yet most of us do it. We don't have to of course. In fact, as this book unfolds you will learn many ways of overcoming this problem.

Let's start with one now. Imagine that you have a **blackboard located somewhere outside of you**, say, off to the right of your head. When something is worrying you, condense whatever it is into a few words and write in on the blackboard. As that worry recurs, keep placing it out on the board rather than letting it stay within your mind. In other words, detach yourself from it, tell yourself you are not your worries. They are something separate from you.

You can extend this idea of detachment to gain a greater sense of control over your life. **Detach yourself from your body, emotions and thoughts** by thinking in the following way:

- Although I have a body, I am not my body. Within a few days, every cell in my body will have changed. This means my body is constantly changing, yet I feel a sense of continuity. Sometimes I am tired; at other times I'm full of energy. Sometimes I feel pain; at other times I experience comfort. With so much change, how is it possible for my identity to be within my body? My body is a vehicle which I use. I am the driver, not the vehicle. Therefore, I am not my body, nor am I my pain or my tiredness.

- In the same way, I can affirm that I am not my emotions. At times I feel miserable, depressed; at other times I am happy, elated, joyous. Because my moods change, my identity cannot be within my passing emotions. I feel but I am not my feelings.
- Nor am I my thoughts. They change so frequently, a constant stream of them flowing through my mind. So my identity is not in my thoughts. I think, but I am not my thoughts. I have an intellect which I can use to solve problems and make decisions, but I am not my intellect.

So I come back to the inner 'I', the essence, which can be imagined as a point of self-awareness. This is the permanent factor in the constantly varying flow of my outer personality. At this point I can observe, direct and harmonize my thoughts, emotions and my body. This means my pain does not lie within me, but within the body. Notice I say 'the' body, not 'my' body. It might be difficult to accept but, if we refuse to accept pain and, instead, place it 'out there' in the body, we can greatly reduce its power to affect us. This is a point that will be elaborated upon in the chapter on healing.

This idea of detachment may be difficult to accept. It seems foreign to our experience but once we train ourselves to behave in this way, we can assume a vastly increased level of control over our lives. Instead of allowing our bodies, our emotions and our thoughts to control us, we control them, and, by so doing, enable ourselves to live the life we want. And isn't this one definition of success, a definition which would be infinitely appealing to many, many people?

However, if the concept of detachment is a bit difficult to accept, perhaps some of the following ideas on managing your emotions may be easier to put into practice.

MANAGING YOUR EMOTIONS

Learning how to manage our emotions more successfully

is likely to qualify as success for most of us. It certainly would for Donald Samuels. Donald, a manager of a small furniture manufacturing business, wants desperately to be less at the mercy of his changing moods, to be less emotionally influenced by people and situations. Quick to anger, Donald reacts adversely to quite innocent remarks, reading into them implications which are competely unintended. He also interprets the remarks of his fellow Rotarians negatively, reacting very sensitively to anything he regarded as a slight.

Yet Donald possesses the power to change all this. He can, if he wishes, modify his attitude. Using the example above, all Donald need do is respond only to the actual words addressed to him. Not the implications he hears, not the innuendos he imagines, just the specific words used. By behaving in this way, Donald would lift a great burden from himself.

In fact, many of us are probably over-sensitive to possible negative undertones in what people say to us. We look for trouble where perhaps none exists. Yet, even if someone is trying to make us feel upset through implying something unpleasant, by reacting only to the actual words spoken we turn off this game.

People who do use innuendo and implication rely on our reacting in a distressed way to these concealed attacks. This is their payoff, making us feel miserable. So if we refuse to respond to hidden messages, acting as if they do not exist, we remove the payoff. When we do this, we no longer provide the desired rewards and, usually, our attacker gives up on us, attempting to find someone else who will show signs of distress when verbally assaulted.

There are other things Donald can do. One of these if to stop creating his own problems. Like many people, he is his own worst enemy. He is, for example, particularly good at **snowballing**. If he has a problem, he allows it to get a firm footing by not facing it when it first appears. Sometimes this works if the problem just vanishes.

Unfortunately, most business problems don't behave like this. They not only remain but escalate unless attended to, and Donald is not good at attending to them. Perhaps he could tell himself '**Do it now**.' Human beings react very strongly to the things they tell themselves so we need to provide positive messages in order to stir us into the action we know we must take.

Unfortunately Donald persists in maintaining a **negative focus for his thinking**. He manages to banish happy thoughts by concentrating on his weaknesses or by convincing himself that other people simply do not understand him. He is very good at blaming himself too, saying 'This is my problem' to many things for which he is not actually responsible. He always assumes the fault is his. Sometimes Donald is right. He has made a mistake. Often he is wrong, and this constant blaming is a big contributor to his negative attitude.

So too is his **expectation that unpleasant things will happen**. Divorced for several years, Donald occasionally goes to parties. Because he expects that he will not enjoy himself, he tends to stand by himself and make little effort to mix with the other guests. Later he complains that no one would talk to him, confirming his original expectation that parties are not enjoyable. Donald has created a self-fulfiling prophecy which, as long as he maintains his negative attitude, will ensure he derives no enjoyment from parties.

Actually, life in general is not all that pleasant for Donald. As part of his attitude of creating his own problems, he **sets goals for himself which are too high**, too difficult to achieve. Naturally enough, he fails to achieve these. This further reinforces his negative view of the world. He sets himself up as a loser in life through choosing to think in ways which are self-destructive and which cause him to feel depressed.

We can usually distinguish the winners in life from the losers by the way they express themselves, for the words we use mirror our attitudes and, to a large extent, control our emotions. In *The Quest for Excellence*, Roly Leopold put it like this.

WINNERS   VERSUS   LOSERS

WINNERS	LOSERS
• Let's find out	• Nobody knows
• I was wrong	• It's not my fault
• I'll make time	• I'm too busy
• Listens	• Waits to talk
• Learns from superiors	• Resents superiors
• There ought to be a better way	• That's the way it has always been done here

---

Winners think, talk and feel positive; losers think, talk, and feel negative. Deliberately changing the way you express yourself will change your attitude. If you don't believe this, do this simple exercise adapted from one used at the Esalen Institute in California.

Choose some aspect of your life towards which you know your mental attitude could be improved and, keeping this in mind, write down and complete the following sentences:

'It's difficult for me to . . .'
'I hope that . . .'
'If I . . . then . . .'
'I'm going to try to . . .'
'I can't . . .'

When you have done this, take a moment to consider what you have written. Notice how the sentences reflect your attitude about the situation. Now rewrite the sentences, amending the first few words as follows:

Replace 'It's difficult for me to . . .' with 'It's a challenge for me to . . .'

> Replace 'I hope that. . .' with 'I know that. . .'
> Replace 'If I . . . then . . .' with 'When I . . .
> then . . .'
> Replace 'I'm going to try to . . .' with 'I'm going
> to . . .'
> Replace 'I can't . . .' with 'I won't . . .'
>
> Notice which of the changes make you feel more posi-
> tive, as if the second version releases new energy into
> the situation you describe and suggests a new way of
> looking at it. Resolve to make these changes when you
> speak about yourself in future, making a conscious
> effort to interrupt and correct your own negative lan-
> guage.

Gaining increased emotional control is really a matter of
listening in so that you become aware of what you tell
yourself. Probably you don't eavesdrop on yourself all
that often but, whether you are aware of it or not, there is
a continual inner dialogue occuring in your head. These
conversations can seriously undermine your peace of mind
for they determine your view of the world. They are the
source of your problems, but they can also be the source
of solutions and change too, so listening in on yourself will
greatly help you to become more self-aware.
    Try the following approach for a week to two so you can
test this out for yourself.

> ● Set aside a few short periods each day in which you
>   simply listen to your inner dialogue. Stop yourself
>   now and then throughout the day, especially when
>   you're faced with a question or problem, and tune in
>   to yourself.
> ● After you have done this for several days, pose some
>   specific topics to yourself such as 'success', 'failure',
>   'old age', 'colds', and listen to what is being said.
> ● You might like to try writing out these 'dialogues'.

- Assume the role of an objective third party and merely listen, attempting not to get involved.
- Make a list of the negative messages you frequently hear yourself making. Realize how these are affecting the ways in which you view the world.
- Make a list of positive counter-arguments to these and feed them into your mind at every opportunity.

Once you become reasonable proficient at doing this you are well on the way to the successful management of your emotions. You will identify the cues or 'buttons' which set off emotional chains of thought and action. As you identify these, they will lose their power over you as you modify your addictions.

ADDICTIONS AND PREFERENCES

In normal conversation when we speak of addictions we mean addiction to things like smoking, alcohol, food, fast cars, and so on. However, they may be seen in another way, one which relates to the idea of emotional control. To discover to what you are addicted, become aware of your anger. When you become angry, this indicates that someone or something is not living up to your expectations. To see how this works in practice, we'll look at how an ex-patient of mine, Joan Cavanagh, was able to achieve the success of taking more control over her emotions and her life in general.

When Joan first consulted me, she was concerned about her inability to handle the pressure engendered by her double role of mother of four children and her job as departmental manager in large store. One symptom she displayed was frequent outbursts of anger. When we started looking at what occasioned these outbursts the same pattern was usually present. Perhaps one of her children was noisy. Joan would explode, shouting at the child to be quiet. Or a salesgirl in the store might make some mistake. Joan's anger would be out of all proportion to the rather trivial nature of the error.

It really came down to **a matter of expectations**. In the first of the above cases, Joan expected her children to be quiet. When they weren't, she became incensed. In the second case, Joan expected her salesgirls never to make mistakes or, in other words, to be perfect. When they were not, she became furious. Rather unreasonable expectations you would say. Joan certainly thought so when the situation was presented to her in this way.

Joan was addicted to her children remaining quiet and to her salesgirls never making mistakes. Joan's husband was addicted to his car always working perfectly. Whenever it refused to start, or gave any trouble at all, he would become very angry. Her mother was addicted to all the household labour-saving devices doing what they were supposed to do. When they gave trouble she was furious.

So, if we want to remove some of the emotional over-reaction from our lives, it would be useful to monitor our anger for this is the sign of an addiction, an often unreasonable expectation which, when violated, occasions an outburst of frustration. When we behave in this way, we are like robots. We don't think about how reasonable or unreasonable our behaviour might be but simply flare up every time our addiction to something happening in a particular way is not met.

This form of behaviour could be termed 'mustitis'. My child *must* be quiet. If he isn't, I just can't stand it. My salesgirls *must* be perfect and when they are not it is just too terrible. This irrational thinking seems rather stupid when set down on paper like this. Yet if you think back over your own behaviour, you'll probably find examples of similar thinking. Often our beliefs are somewhat rigid and, when they are, addictions are rampant.

The answer is to replace addictions with preferences. Easier said than done, but not impossible. Joan could choose to think in this way. I would prefer it if my children were quiet, but it is unlikely, given the nature of children, that they will be. I'd better flow with it rather than blowing up and making both myself and my children feel bad. I don't achieve anything by my anger. It doesn't make them quieter, except maybe very temporarily, so I'm achieving nothing positive. In fact I'm getting all emotional and possibly damaging myself by the fierceness of my reaction.

Similarily she could choose to think that, though it would be nice if her salesgirls were unnerringly accurate, they are only human and therefore prone to make mistakes. Her anger is unlikely to change that situation. It will, in all likelihood, damage her relations with her staff. There are no positive gains, only negative emotional reactions.

If we could, each year, turn even one of our addictions into a preference, gradually we would become successful in achieving much greater control over our emotions. This seems well worth the effort for we will then be able to more readily accept others as they are instead of how we think they ought to be. It will also remove some of the need we have to manipulate others into doing the things we think they ought to do.

MANIPULATION

When we were very young, our parents manipulated us, usually through fear and guilt, to do what they felt we ought to do. This could be positive in that we were being protected, prevented from doing things which could harm us. It could also be negative in that we were being forced to act in ways which were not in our best interests. Whether our parents used fear and guilt to protect us or not, a legacy is carried forward such that we are susceptible to manipulation later in life.

Consider Colin and Rhonda Thompson. Colin is on his way out of the door for his Saturday game of golf when Rhonda says: 'The children were saying this morning that they hardly ever see you'. The intention of this statement is to create, within Colin, a sense of guilt. He is letting down his children. He is deficient as a father. Perhaps, as a result, he stays home which is what Rhonda desired.

Because she didn't want to ask him to do this directly, she became manipulative, playing on his guilt feelings. But a person cannot be made to feel guilty unless he or she cooperates. In this case, Colin cooperated.

On other occasions there could be a reversal with Rhonda, as a result of her earlier conditioning to fear, being manipulated into behaving as Colin wished. Perhaps he might want her to accompany him on an overnight trip. Rhonda isn't interested. To effect a change in her decision, Colin reminds her of how frightened she becomes when he is away at night. Rhonda decides she had better go along after all.

Together with fear and guilt, selfishness is another label useful in the manipulation game. Because most of us are brought up to be unselfish, to put our own interests behind those of others, we are vulnerable to the charge of being 'selfish'. Using the example of Colin going off to his golf game, Rhonda could have said: 'You're so selfish playing golf when we could go shopping together.' This is really only a variant of guilt-inducement, but the label does carry a lot of power in itself. The interesting point is that Colin could, with equal validity, accuse his wife of being 'selfish' in wanting him to go shopping. She probably wouldn't see it that way though.

In my therapy practice, I see many people in their 30s and 40s who are frustrated through having subordinated their wishes to spouses and children and now feel like doormats—unappreciated and ignored. It does not seem 'selfish' for people to explore their own interests, some of the time at least, instead of always putting these interests last. Yet, many do not do so through the power of that word 'selfish'.

This is not to say that we should always put ourselves first. Some form of balance is needed. However, what I am saying is that, unless we become aware of how we are susceptible to manipulation, we can find ourselves doing many things in our lives which may not be in our best interests.

This self-awareness is necessary if we are not to take over as our own the problems of someone else. Recently, after being interviewed on a radio programme, I was having lunch with some colleagues, one of whom objected violently to what I had said, believing I was over-simplifying psychology and, by so doing, undermining the profession. When I asked him precisely what I had said that was so damaging, he was unable to tell me, continuing to talk in very general terms. Despite continued questioning I was unable to get any clear indication of where, in his eyes, I was going wrong. Finally I said something like: 'I'm sorry what I said upset you but I really believe in the things I was talking about. So I think it is you who has the problem rather than me.'

This hardly endeared me to him but I think we can too readily accept someone else's problem as our own. Many of the patients I see have done this, particularly those with sexual problems. I find again and again that the wrong person has come along. It is the partner at home who really has the problem but has been able to convince his or her spouse differently.

In situations when a person is attempting to convince you that the difficulty is yours, be prepared to ask direct questions to clarify the issue. Keep probing to find out exact what the trouble is, then you can do something about resolving it. However, if the other person is unable to provide such clarification, he or she is probably reacting very emotionally because you have inadvertently violated one of his or her pet prejudices. In this case, all you can really do is point out that the problem is not yours so you don't intend to do anything about it.

Through increased self-awareness, it does become increasingly easy to identify when you are being manipulated. You can also become aware of when you are manipulating others. Althought I have been using the word 'manipulation' rather negatively, it can also have a positive connotation as when parents attempt to prevent their children doing potentially harmful things.

If you use manipulation to create positive outcomes for others and for yourself, increased self-awareness should enable to you become more successful at this. On the other hand, if you are using manipulation in a negative way, to force others into doing things which are not in their best interests, increased knowledge of this gives you the opportunity to modify this behaviour, perhaps to eliminate it.

Nowhere is this understanding more valuable than in the art of selling. Persuading others to buy what you are offering, be it yourself, your ideas, or your products, is basically a process of manipulation. This is equally true when it is you who are on the receiving end of the selling interaction. So becoming more aware of persuasive selling practices can contribute substantially to your success in life.

3 Success in Selling

PERSUASIVE SELLING

In an excellent book entitled *Modern Persuasion Strategies*, Moine and Herd describe a number of interesting selling techniques. The first of these they call **instant replay**. It involves finding what the customer considers important when he or she contemplates a purchase.

A woman—we'll call her Helen—is shopping for a new microwave oven. The salesman approaches her and learns which appliance is the object of her interest. He then inquires about her present stove, asking her why she bought that particular model. Helen tells him that she liked the solidarity of the stove, the impression of quality that it conveyed. That was the main factor influencing her decision to buy, the price and the stove's appearance being of lesser importance. Armed with this information, the salesman concentrates on quality, price, and appearance in that order as he suggests various microwave models to Helen. She has virtually told him how she wants to be sold.

The same approach can be used when attempting to sell a product to a firm which is already being supplied by a competitor. Rather than criticize the existing supplier, which is usually a counter-productive ploy, more success is likely to come from asking: 'If you had to make a change, what would you want that your present supplier doesn't offer?' Once again, the salesman is asking the potential customer to give him the information he needs in order to make a successful sale. And it works. By asking the appropriate questions, people will tell you the criteria they use in making a purchase. All you need do is replay that information, applying it to the current potential purchase.

A second technique is that of **mental hinging**. When you use this approach you link undeniably true statements to what you want your customer to experience next. The words which create these links range in strength quite markedly.

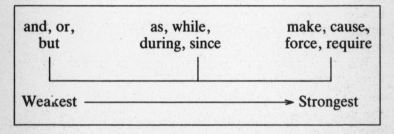

and, or, but	as, while, during, since	make, cause, force, require

Weakest ———————————————→ Strongest

The weakest link words (and, or, but) are best used early in the sales presentation: 'You are standing here looking at this water pump *and* you can picture how it will improve your mining operation'. Use stronger words (as, while, during, since) in the middle of the interaction: '*As* you have worked out how to operate the pump, go ahead and start it'. For the close, employ the strongest link words (make, cause, require): 'This pump is so powerful that it *makes* you want to buy it'. Gradually increasing the strength of the linkages you make is a subtle way of leading the customer into making the purchase.

Subtlety is present in the next technique, too, which Moine refers to as using **mental erasers**. These are simply words which erase information, and their use leaves it up to the customer to fill in the specifics which have been left out. Advertising virtually depends on such erasers as can be seen from the following table.

ERASER TYPE	EXAMPLES	INFORMATION ERASED
-ly	clearly certainly	Clear to whom? What makes it certain?
-er -est	faster, slower prettiest	Compared to what? What makes it so?
less, more least, most	less expensive more efficient	Compared to what? What makes it so?

This is a very successful sales technique. If you do not already use it, try it out. You will be delighted with the results. Also, by becoming aware of its somewhat insidious nature, you will be better armed to resist when someone else uses it on you.

Words certainly can have tremendous power, either through their omission, as demonstrated above, or through their use to influence emotions and feelings as in the next persuasive sales technique, **triggers**. For many people, a sentence such as 'Discover our new taste treat,' triggers off a favourable response. This is due to conditioning for, as we grow up, certain words come to have powerful effects on us. Words such as 'new', 'natural', 'light', 'save', 'free', 'rich', 'real', 'fresh', 'extra', 'discover' normally evoke positive connotations, so their use is likely to increase the influence of a sales presentation.

A rather subtle way in which triggers may be used is to get a customer feeling good early in a sales interaction. This might be done by asking about a favourite sport or hobby, inquiring about a recent holiday, or being complementary on some aspect of his or her appearance. When you observe a look of pleasure, say in a special tone something like: 'That's terrific', widen your eyes, nod, and tap with a pencil. Later, use these same words together with the eye widening, nodding, and pencil tapping to evoke that same sense of pleasure within the customer.

Once you become aware of a customer's triggers, you

can copy them. Notice what they do when they are feeling good. Perhaps they give a short laugh, rub their chin, or turn up their mouth at the corners. Later you can use those cues yourself. Laugh in the same way, rub your chin, let your mouth turn up, and you will reinstate the happiness in the customer. Happy customers are more likely to buy than those who are miserable.

Using words in a more commanding way can be very persuasive, too. The **hidden action commands** approach involves using a different tone of voice to emphasize certain words. Looking directly at a customer, speaking firmly and deliberately, you could say: 'I don't know if you'll *buy this car, Fred*,' stressing the last four words.

Instead of the positive approach in which you tell the customer, with as much subtlety as possible, what he or she should do, you might like to try **negative selling**. This technique is embodied in a statement such as: 'Of course, Ron, you really don't need a training programme. You're already so successful.' Faced with such a comment, the other person may then proceed to argue against your statement, and convince himself he needs your programme.

This is role reversal. You can actually challenge your customer by saying: 'Given your situation, why would you want what I have to offer?' Many people will sell themselves when given an opportunity like this.

They will also provide their own solutions. Take the case of an irate ratepayer coming into the Council Chambers to complain about some perceived injustice. The mistake, so easy to make, is to argue with this person. That simply throws fuel on the flames. The more you argue, the more irate the ratepayer will become.

However, if you listen in silence, he or she will soon run out of words. Then you can use the rapport engendering response of: 'If I was in your shoes I'd probably feel exactly the same. What do you think should be done about this?' By creating a sense of rapport, you will defuse the ratepayer's anger, and, by requesting a solution to the point at issue, you often get a ready-made solution which is usually easy to implement.

This is a type of **refocusing** technique. Other ways of encouraging a change of viewpoint, a perception of things from a different angle, are to ask questions such as: 'What would happen if. . .?' or 'Just suppose. . .' By having customers look at things in ways different from the usual, you help them open up to possibilities they may not have considered before. This would be important if you wanted them to change from one product, handled by a competitor, to the one you are selling.

When you want to accomplish such a change, using the **repeated 'yes'** can help a great deal. This is the process of making statements that are undeniably true and turning them into questions such as: 'We all do things for our own good reasons, don't we?' Virtually anything a client says may be reformulated into a question designed to elicit a 'yes': 'You said your company is very concerned about the happiness of your employees?' Obvious generalizations can be turned into questions very easily: 'We all feel happy about a bargain, don't we?' Simply repeating what a customer says while nodding your head in affirmation works well too: 'You like it?' , 'You agree with me?', 'The colour is the one you like?'

A final persuasive selling technique is that of **bridging**, which is a matter of pacing the customer's present focus of attention. Use all communication channels, moving smoothly between the visual, auditory, and kinesthetic sensory modes until you identify which of these is the one preferred by the customer. By focusing on this, you increase your chances of making a sale for all of us do seem to have a favoured way of representing our experience.

REPRESENTATIONAL SYSTEMS

In our minds we represent our experiences, ideas and thinking in certain ways. Rather than a real world existing within our heads, we have representations of that world which provide a sort of map of our experience. As we see, hear and feel things from the external world, we store or represent them in our minds. Later, we are able to recall these sights, sounds and feelings just as we originally experienced them.

The words we use are derived from these representations, so that our thinking and communication is affected by which of the three basic representational systems we are employing. Though we use all systems,—visual, auditory and kinesthetic (feeling)—most of us tend to favour one over the others. This means we can take a particular representational system or combination of systems as being the way a person thinks, enabling us to tailor our communication to match that system. By so doing we increase both rapport and the chance that our communication will be clearly understood.

There are a number of ways of identifying a person's representational system. Some of these are rather subtle and difficult to use. There are, however, two which can provide the required information relatively easily. The first is a matter of taking notice of the words people use, for the choice they make indicates the particular system they are employing.

Visual	Auditory	Kinesthetic
see	tune	feel
look	hear	touch
picture	listen	rough
bright	loud	cold
imagine	say	grasp
clear	sound	handle

If a person uses words from one of these groups more than from the other two, it suggests he or she communicates best in that particular system. That person will understand, and be more powerfully influenced, by ideas you express in the same system because you will be speaking his or her language.

The second relatively simple way of identifying some-one's favourite representational system involves taking note of his or her eye movements. Most people have a consistent pattern of eye movements which reflect the particular system of though he or she is using. Looking up indicates visual representation, looking to the side or down to the left suggests the auditory mode, while looking down to the right identifies the kinesthetic representation.

Though most of the people you meet will have such a pattern, individuals do differ. A left-handed person, for example, may have the sides reversed. However, he or she will still be consistent, in that visual, auditory, and kinesthetic will always be in the same place for each person. So, once you identify the system being used through observation of eye movements, this pattern will remain constant for that person.

Other ways of tapping into another person's representational system are through the observation of breathing patterns, pitch of voice and speech patterns. All these are channels of communication.

COMMUNICATION CHANNELS

VISUALS

- Eye movements—up, pan left to right
- Language—'appears', 'bird's eye view'
- Breath—high up in chest
- Voice—high pitched
- Speech—rapid bursts

●●● USE VISUAL WORDS: 'Can you see what I mean?'
USE VISUAL AIDS

AUDITORY

- Eye movements—left and down

- Body language—hand touches face, rubs chin, telephone position, chin in hand
- Language—'clear as a bell', 'tuned in'

●●● USE AUDITORY WORDS: 'Listen to the way these doors latch. Hardly audible'

ACTION-FEELING

- Eye movements—right and down
- Language—'come to grips with', 'fall apart'
- Breath—full and deep
- Speech—slow with gestures
- Voice—low and resonant

●●● USE ACTION-FEELING WORDS—'Feel the luxury of the seats'
HAVE THEM DO THINGS, TOUCH, OPERATE

As well as looking up as they speak and using words such as: 'I've got a clear picture of this now', visualizers tend to breathe high up in their chests, and speak rapidly in a relatively high pitched voice.

Kinesthetics look down to the right, comment that they 'really have a grip of things now', breathe deeply, and speak slowly in a resonant voice. Those favouring the auditory mode look sideways or down to the left, and, while touching their faces, say things like: 'That's as clear as a bell to me now.'

Because you build trust and rapport through pacing or matching a person's representational system, it is certainly worth the effort expended in gaining a knowledge of the relevant cues. In fact, speaking in terms of a person's language preference is probably the fastest way to build trust. Other ways of doing so including matching mood states, body language, breathing rhythm, voice volume and rate of speech.

The key to successful pacing is to realize that everyone

thinks he or she is normal. Therefore, if someone to whom you are speaking talks very slowly and deliberately, that is what he or she considers normal. If you speak quickly, they are inclined to think you are somewhat peculiar. To establish rapport with such a person, slow down your speech.

Similarly, if you are bouncy, bubbly and bright when talking to someone who is feeling low and miserable, you are not likely to get far. Not that I suggest you become depressed to pace that person better. Simply tone down a little so the contrast is not so marked. Incidentally, this is why telling someone who is low to 'cheer up' is usually so ineffective. First pace their mood, then you may be able to help them feel better. You might even be able to help them handle rejection better.

HANDLING REJECTION

One of the most soul-destroying aspects of selling is the rejection which comes with the job. No one, no matter how successful, is going to win all the time and, when rejection is frequent, self-esteem suffers greatly, sometimes to the extent that a form of paralysis sets in. The salesperson becomes afraid to try and sell.

To overcome this syndrome, it is necessary to think in ways which do not lead to a negative mental attitude. In *How to Master the Art of Selling*, Tom Hopkins suggests that failure should never be seen as failure but only as:

- an opportunity to learn;
- the negative feedback you need to change course in a more positive direction;
- the opportunity to develop your sense of humour by laughing at your errors as soon as possible after you have made them;
- an opportunity to practice your techniques and perfect your performance.

Another useful approach is to determine the cash value of each rejection your receive. For example, each time you make a sale you may receive a commission of $100. Work out how many people you usually need to contact in order to close a sale. Perhaps, this number is ten. Therefore, each contact is worth $10. Think of being paid not by the sale but by the contact. For every genuine contact with whom you do not close a sale, you are earning $10. Every time you hear a 'no', you earn what you have worked out as the cash value per contact.

If you secure one sale out of every ten contacts, you can choose to think of every 'no' as bringing you that much closer to a 'yes'. Selling is a percentage game, so that those who risk many rejections by working with many people, are likely to make a lot of money. That is because the key to making more money is to see more people.

After a rejection, never stop there. Always make more calls until you achieve a success. Never stop on a losing note. This is akin to the advice given people when they fall off a horse. Get back on immediately. The longer you delay, the harder it is to get started again. After all, it is not the number of times we fail that matters, but the number of times that we succeed, and this success rate is directly proportional to the number of times we fail but keep on trying.

That could be the moral of this book. We don't have to accept failure. Within us we have the power to be successful, however we care to define that term. Success is primarily a function of how we choose to think, but without self-awareness we lack the knowledge upon which to base such choice. However, all the self-awareness in the world avails for nothing if we do not practise the self-discipline of putting into practice what we have learnt about ourselves.

4 Self-Discipline

ACCEPTING PERSONAL RESPONSIBILITY

The key issue involved in self-discipline is taking responsibility for what happens to us rather than blaming people and situations outside ourselves. Those who are successful realize that, to a very great extent, they are responsible for shaping their own destiny. It is not events which shape our lives so much as our opinion of those events.

Most people pose the question: 'What is making me unsuccessful?' rather than the far more fruitful one: 'What am I doing to make myself unsuccessful?' The first question places our fate in the hands of others. The second, because it makes us responsible for our own success, motivates us more highly to stir ourselves into action.

It is possible to see life as a series of events which may be expanded or contracted. Tony Smallwood has done the former. His first business venture, a newsagency, failed. Seven years later, he is still talking about this failure, reciting in great detail all the things which, through no fault of his own, went wrong. Unlike others who have encountered similar failures, learned from them, and put them aside, Tony has taken this event and expanded it so it continues to fill part of his life. Instead of letting it die, he has kept it alive.

Julie Matthews has behaved quite differently. An editor of a country newspaper, Julie was injured in a car accident, becoming a paraplegic. She nows 'writes' children's books by dictating her material into a tape recorder. Julie is an extremely cheerful and productive person who has choosen to contract an extremely negative event so that she can get on with her life. People who do not know her well believe she 'puts on' a brave face. Her friends are constantly amazed at her positive attitude towards life. Instead of expanding the past, she has, as far as possible, cast it aside.

Perhaps, as Molière has stated, things are worth what we make them worth. Again we see that it is the attitute we choose to take to events which is of more importance than the events themselves. This simple truth, which lies at the heart of successful living, is a basic premise of a therapeutic approach pioneered by Albert Ellis.

RATIONAL-EMOTIVE THERAPY

In its basic form, Ellis's technique is as simple as ABC. A is the activating event, B is a person's belief system, thoughts and attitudes, and C is the emotional consequences. Applying this system to Tony's situation we get:

A—Failure of his business.
B—'This should not happen to me, it is terrible, awful, catastrophic.'
C—Constant blaming of others, anger, distress.

As far as Julie's case is concerned, it would read like this:

A—Crippling car accident.
B—'No use crying over spilt milk. Let's make the most of what I've got left.'
C—Cheerful optimism.

So it is not, as most people assume, that A, the activating event, causes C, the emotional response. Between these two comes B, the belief structure of the person involved, for it is this structure which determines what the response will be. Tony 'awfulizes', blowing his event up out of all proportion to its seriousness. Thus his emotional reaction is a very negative one. Julie minimizes the importance of her event. Her reaction is, accordingly, far more positive.

Ellis's therapy involves disputation over beliefs, his intention being to help people modify their thinking so that it becomes more rational. When this happens, they modify their emotional reactions to the events in their lives and, by so doing, handle their lives more successfully. Let's see how this approach can be applied to a business situation.

Arthur Gregson is sales manager of a firm marketing automotive parts. He is to attend an executive meeting which, as one item on its agenda, will be considering sales performance over the previous three months. If Arthur thinks irrationally he will be talking to himself thus:

> 'I just *have* to acquit myself well at this meeting. I *must* succeed in convincing the others that I am doing everything I can to halt the sales slide. It is *absolutely imperative* that I impress that on everyone. It would be *awful* if I failed to do so. I'll be a *complete failure*, and I *can't stand* that.'

On the other hand, if he is a more rational person, he will talk to himself in somewhat different terms:

> 'It is important that I acquit myself well at this meeting. I'll prepare thoroughly so I give myself every chance of convincing the others that I have done everything I can to halt the sales slide. I want to impress that on everyone. I would be pretty disappointed if I couldn't do so. It would seem that I'd failed to achieve the goals set. I'll have to live with that, learn from what has gone wrong over the past three months, and do better next quarter.'

There are some important differences between these two ways of self-talk. In particular, when he thinks irrationally, Arthur:

- *demands* that he performs well and *insists* that he must not fail;
- *exaggerates* the consequences of failure;
- *puts himself down.*

This overreacting relates to a point made earlier, that things are worth what we make them worth. The irrational thinker exaggerates the importance of events, then tells himself it would be a catastrophy to fail. He has many other beliefs which are similarily unreasonable. Ellis has listed many of these in his best known work, *A Guide to Rational Living*. Some of the more common are:

- 'I must be loved and/or approved of by everyone I know.'
- 'I must do everything perfectly.'
- 'When things don't go my way it is horrible.'
- 'I have no control over my emotions and whatever unhappiness befalls me.'
- 'If something is threatening, I must worry about it constantly.'
- 'There is no way to overcome the past; it determines my present behaviour.'
- 'People and events should turn out in a positive way, and if they don't it's awful.'

People who think like this need, according to Ellis, to have their beliefs constantly challenged and disputed. A useful way of doing so is to pose the following questions: 'What would happen if it/they didn't?', 'If you don't do everything perfectly, what would happen?' or 'If something is threatening, what would happen if you didn't worry about it?' This is one way of helping people recognize and perhaps do something about their irrational thinking. There are other ways, too.

CONTROLLING YOUR THOUGHTS

When we look at how we might combat irrational thinking we return to the issue of exerting some control over what we think about. We act as if every thought which comes into our minds must be pursued. This is not so. You have the power to choose. Perhaps you may care to imagine that your mind is a room which has an open window either side. Thoughts are like birds, they fly in through one window and out through the other. We can watch them pass without the necessity of considering them further. However, when a thought which you want to pursue flies into your mind, shut the windows, keep the thought there, and develop it at will.

Alternatively, you might consider your mind as if it was a pond, the surface of which is incredibly still, like glass. Above the water is the conscious part of your mind. Below the surface lies the unconscious. As a thought comes into your mind, watch it rise like a stream of bubbles from the bottom of the pond. When it reaches the surface, if it is not a thought you wish to consider further, let it burst into nothingness. Of course, if you want to develop the thought, imagine the bubble expanding out to fill the conscious mind, the area above the surface.

Perhaps you might like to go on a mental diet. We often diet to improve our physical selves. A similar approach, used to improve our mental selves, is equally valid. When we awake each morning we are given a marvellous gift for, as Bertrand Russell has said, 'Every day is a new life to a wise man.' For this one day, do not entertain a negative thought. This means that, should such a thought come into our minds, we do not allow it to remain. As the Chinese proverb has it: 'We cannot stop the birds of sorrow from flying over our heads, but we can stop them from nesting in our hair.'

If you are not as successful in following this diet as you would like, don't despair. You have a new life coming up next day providing a fresh start. When you do achieve a day of successful mental dieting, add a second day to it, then a third and a fourth. By refusing to think negatively, you lift a load of worry from your shoulders.

Worry, which can be defined as over-concern, is very much an aspect of irrational thinking. As one cynical observer of the human scene commented: 'The reason why worry kills more people than work is that more people worry than work.' Worrying and success do not usually go hand in hand, so it is useful to look as some ways of helping yourself avoid this pitfall, as set out below.

TO SHRINK YOUR WORRIES

- **Question it**—Is it really your problem? Are you taking on yourself the problems of other people and treating them as your own?
- **Talk it out**—Share your worry with someone else. It never seems as bad when you bring it out into the open.
- **Write it out**—When you put something on paper it is far easier to see it in perspective.
- **Shrug it off**—Do this literally. Raise then droop your shoulders. It is a very effective way to relax.
- **Breathe it away**—Inhale deeply, exhale with a sigh, letting go your worry with the breath.
- **Set a worry session**—Set aside a specific time, say 15 minutes to do nothing else but worry.
- **Work it off**—Do something physical which absorbs your total attention if possible.
- **Laugh it off**—Look for some humour in the situation, even if the laugh is on you.
- **Distance it**—Will whatever you are worrying about really matter a few years from now?
- **Balance it**—Find a good side to it as well as a bad.
- **Exaggerate it**—Picture the worst. Is it likely to happen?
- **Hold it**—Say 'Stop', pause, take a fresh look at whatever is worrying you.

- **Escape it**—Shift attention away by noticing something enjoyable around you.
- **Attack it**—Take the first step in solving the problem.
- **Assert yourself for it**—Say 'No' when you need to.
- **Plan for it**—Get up earlier to prepare for it.

All these techniques are really ways of interrupting irrational over-concern, and going off in a new direction. We become good worriers by constant practising. To break this habit, we need to set up another habit which conflicts with the first one. Every time we catch ourselves worrying uselessly over something, we can deliberately interrupt until we create a habit of behaving in this way. It takes a lot of effort to worry, and, by interrupting that activity, we release a lot of energy. This can be devoted to activities more likely to contribute to our success.

Through the use of worry-reduction techniques, it becomes easier to flow with life. Such flow might well be the essence of wisdom. For all of us, life does have its undesirable aspects. Nothing is completely satisfactory all of the time. The wise person accepts the immediate difficulty as one of life's negative events which happens to be, just for the moment, facing him or her.

At such a time, it is sensible to ask ourselves: 'Can I change this for the better? If so, how?' Sometimes we can make changes. At other times we cannot. Then it is necessary to accept the fact that many things we do not like cannot be changed. It is useless to worry about these events, or to catastrophize about them irrationally. Flow with them, let them pass without expanding them into something which will make life miserable.

Of course, there are actions we can take to improve our life situation despite living in a world where undesirable events exist. Within the pages of this book, many such actions are described in terms of how they may help you live more successfully. In some way or another, most of these relate to three key themes which epitomize **the essence of wisdom**.

- Use calm mental rehearsal of future events to engender greater success. This topic is considered fully in the next chapter.
- Become more accepting, non-judgemental compassionate and loving towards ourselves and others.
- Emphasize the positive aspects and potentials of ourselves and others.

Janice Everington put this third idea into practice in a very successful way. Together with several other people, she was employed as a researcher for a television talk programme. Unfortunately, she disliked one of her collegues greatly. Because she had to work and be with him for several hours each day, enjoyment of her job diminshed greatly. This was a problem she raised with me during a course I was conducting.

I suggested that Janice reframe the way she was looking at the situation. This she could do by considering the idea that, rather than disliking her collegue, Ted, she actually disliked the image of him she had in her mind. When we meet someone for the first time, we react either favourably or unfavourably, depending on the associations the person rouses within us. This initial opinion then becomes a filter through which we interpret further impressions. If we reacted unfavourably on first meeting, in the future we tend to concentrate on negative rather than positive things about that person. Often we simply overlook the strengths, seeing only the weaknesses.

So Janice determined that, for a period of two weeks, she would deliberately look for positive aspects in Ted while ignoring the negative ones. Everyone has good and bad features, so Janice became increasingly aware that she hadn't been very fair in her opinion of Ted. Though he could be annoying in many ways, Janice realized he was a conscientious worker, he often helped out the other researchers if they had a problem, and he had quite a dry sense of humour. Though she did not become particularly friendly with Ted, her previous very negative reaction to him was greatly modified so he was no longer a threat to her job enjoyment. In fact, she felt much calmer at work than she had for a long time, and a sense of calmness is important for our general wellbeing.

CALMING THE MIND

In simple terms, most of our agitation stems from thoughts which cause us to feel upset. Therefore, as with interrupting worry, we need to deliberately shift our minds away from that which is upsetting us to something which is more calming. Mantras serve such a function. The sanskrit word, **mantra**, is derived from *man* (mind) and *tra* (protect), thus it means a sound which protects us from the mind. Many mantras have been tested and handed down through the ages, perhaps the most powerful of these being 'Om Namah Shivaya' (pronounced 'om numaa shivaa-yuh') which means 'I honour my own inner state'. This mantra, like any other, is continually repeated, its effect being to create a sense of inner stillness, contentment and enjoyment. The more it is used, the more effective it becomes. In fact, the most vehement adherents of this approach claim that use of a mantra provides the key to perfect inner health. It is suggested that half an hour every day should be spent practising this technique with eyes shut, and, in addition, with eyes open, it should be repeated whenever possible during the day.

Initially I was very sceptical about the claims made for any particular mantra. This was because I had read several scientific studies which 'proved' that there existed no particular power in the sacred Eastern mantras, and that repetition of any word, such as one's own name or the number 'one', would produce comparable results.

However, as I continued to read of the results achieved by people who were using 'Om Namah Shivaya' to calm themselves during times of pressure, I decided to try it myself. As I have suggested in previous books, you have to be your own expert, finding what works for you. This particular mantra has worked well for me. It has also helped Matthew Carter. Matthew, who runs a real estate company, suffered from high blood pressure and ulcers. A rather impatient man, he was always rushing, attempting to do several different things at the same time. When first he consulted me, Matthew was willing to try anything which might help him slow down and relax. However, my suggestion of the mantra was greeted with derision. He simply didn't have time for such foolery. A common attitude this, unfortunately. Before he even made any attempt to find out if the technique would help him, he dismissed it as 'rubbish'.

However, through a stroke of good fortune, his son, whom he had not seen for many years, came to visit him. Matthew was rather surprised to find that his son was practising transcendental meditation. He had always regarded his son as much like himself, hard headed, practical and a real go-getter. If his son found this rather odd technique useful, perhaps it might be worth looking into.

Though he never really stuck to his daily half-hour practice, Matthew did use the mantra during his daily activities when he felt agitated and pressured. For example, he was a man who hated to wait in queues, thinking of this as a waste of valuable time. As a result, he would become very impatient under such circumstances, ready to 'blow up' as he put it, a condition not helpful to alleviating either the high blood pressure or the ulcer. So, instead of fuming at the delay, Matthew repeated the mantra over and over again. Much to his surprise, he felt calmer almost immediately and it was not long before he was actually looking for opportunities to use the mantra. After behaving in this way for six months, his blood pressure had dropped and his ulcers no longer bothered him.

Not everyone gains such benefits, but most people who use some form of mantra to calm themselves when they are under pressure attest to its value. So, too, do those who use a simple Zen breathing technique which I first described in *The Plus Factor*.

Without attempting to alter it in any way, observe your breathing. As you inhale, imagine the number 1 in the third eye position at the base of your nose. As you exhale, imagine this number sinking down to your body centre located just below your navel. As your next breath comes in, 'see' the number 2 in the third eye position and, as the breath flows out, take it down beside the number 1. Follow the same procedure until you reach 10. Should you lose count, start again. Possibly several sets of 10 may be necessary before you reach the desired state of calm, but reach it you probably will. Incidentally, this particular technique is also an excellent pain reliever, a point which will be elaborated upon later in the chapter on healing.

Allowing thoughts to flow through your mind without attempting to develop or follow them has already been mentioned. The sense of detachment engendered by adopting this attitude is an excellent way of inducing a state of tranquillity. So, too, is imagining your mind as if it is blue sky disturbed only by several clouds representing problems. See the clouds being burnt away by the sun until only the clear blueness remains. As this occurs, there is usually an increased sense of tranquillity.

Success, as we have seen, means different things to different people. However, if the participants who attend my management courses and the clients who come seeking therapeutic help are any indication, many see the achievement of a calm mind as one of the great successes to which they aspire. It requires self-discipline to succeed in this way. It also requires considerable self-discipline to achieve personal freedom in an unfree world.

ACHIEVING MORE PERSONAL FREEDOM

In a book entitled *How I Found Freedom in an Unfree World*, Harry Brown suggests that free people have four distinguishing characteristics. These are all embodied in a car-rental-firm executive of my acquaintance. This man, I'll call him Ray Cowen, has adopted an attitude to life which has made him the envy of others who lack the courage to follow their convictions. Ray really enjoys life. He feels that his success in both his business and his personal life is primarily due to his adoption of Brown's principles.

The first of these is to **choose positively rather than negatively**. What many people do, when faced by a number of alternatives, is to choose the one which will cause the least discomfort. Their fear of making waves causes them to play safe and not go for the alternative which would be more likely to enhance their lives. Not so Ray. The question he asks himself is: 'Which of these alternatives would make me happiest?' The difference between these two attitudes is really that between the opimist and the pessimist. It has been said that the optimist is wrong about as often as is the pessimist, but that he or she has a lot more fun. It certainly works out that way for Ray.

He also adheres strongly to Brown's second principle which is to **choose direct alternatives**. Attempting to be as realistic as possible, Ray looks at a particular situation and asks himself: 'With things as they are, what can I do *by myself* to make things better?' This is in direct contrast to many unsuccessful people who attempt to get what they want by working indirectly through other people. They ask a different question: 'Who must be changed so that I can achieve the thing I want?' and join groups of people apparently after the same things. In theory this should be a good move for surely a group can exert more pressure than an individual. The problem is that the person joining a group has first to convince the other members to do what he wants. He may spend a lot of time trying to do this, often getting nowhere because the other members, he finds, are usually not as like-minded as he first thought.

Ray has no such problems. Rather than waste energy on trying to convince others to make a common front, he focuses his resources on doing those things which are within his own power. Usually he goes about it quietly, not 'throwing his weight around', but determinedly driving towards the goal he has set himself. He seems to get what he wants with remarkable regularity and does so without offending others to any great extent.

Brown's philosophy is basically a selfish one in that his emphasis lies on the individual rather than on groups. Thus, his views would be quite unacceptable to those who advocate drastic changes in society as being necessary before any real freedom is possible. With Brown, Ray believes that we could grow old waiting for society to change and that it is more productive for the individual to look after his own destiny as far as possible. Accordingly, he chooses to **become involved in those situations which suit him**, rather than those which do not.

We are constantly pressured to take up various 'causes', all of which tend to be very time consuming. If adopting 'causes' provides you with a sense of fulfilment and satisfaction, then this seems a sensible course to adopt. You must be selective however, for the world is full of people who believe you 'should', 'ought', 'must' become involved in their particular 'cause'. By yielding to such pressure, you will have little time left to pursue your own individual goals which, presumably, spell success to you. If the 'causes' move you towards the achievement of these goals, join them by all means. If they don't, you are better off leaving them alone.

Ray does leave them alone. This makes him less than popular with some people who extol the virtue of involvement in social issues, yet he says that he really wouldn't be comfortable with such people. Sounds very self-centred doesn't it? Yet, it actually makes a lot of sense, for Brown's fourth principle is that free individuals choose to **reveal themselves as they really are**, rather than adopting roles which they think make them more acceptable. As Ray maintains, if he pretended to be someone that he wasn't, he would attract people to him in whom he would not really be interested. By showing himself openly as he is, Ray finds others who are similar. It would be easy to say that he would therefore have fewer close relationships, but that is not the case. Maybe there are lots of people around who warm to someone willing to be himself.

So, in short, Ray chooses:

- positively rather than negatively,
- direct alternatives,
- to be involved only in situations which suit him,
- to reveal himself as he actually is.

For him, it seems to work very well. Blatant selfishness perhaps, yet Ray is a person to whom many others turn for help in times of trouble, help which he gives freely. Basically he has choosen to become master of his own time, by going directly towards the things he wants rather than being sidetracked by playing the roles and games society thinks appropriate. That seems a pretty good definition of at least one form of success because Ray has been able to avoid most of society's 'traps'. These, according to Brown, bind people in chains.

You may or may not agree that the following chart indicates 'traps' but the concept will, I hope, cause you to think a little about your own behaviour.

THE CHAINS THAT BIND

- The Identity Trap
  —you should live in a way determined by others
  —other people react to things as you do
- The Intellect-Emotion Trap
  —your intellect tells you what you should feel
  —you can make important decisions when you are strongly emotional
- The Morality Trap
  —you must obey a moral code created by others
  —doing what is 'right' is more important than your happiness
- The Unselfishness Trap
  —you must put the happiness of others ahead of your own

- The Group Trap
    —you can accomplish more in a group than you can acting alone
- The Utopia Trap
    —you must create better conditions in society before you can be free
    —there are compelling social issues in which you must participate
- The Despair Trap
    —other people and circumstances can prevent you being free

Some readers will agree and some disagree with Brown's philosophy. The choice is yours whether you attempt to implement his ideas as Ray has done. Should you desire to change in the ways he suggests, or in any other way for that matter, the concept of self-motivation becomes important.

5 Self-Motivation

BE YOUR OWN BEST FRIEND

If you are to motivate yourself successfully, one way to begin is by becoming your own best friend. Good friends provide encouragement, sound advice, inspiration, and kind words. These are indeed great blessings, blessings which you can learn to bestow upon yourself.

It is important to be helpful to yourself. Too often you may talk to yourself in very destructive ways, destroying self-motivation rather than creating it. It is probable that you say things like 'I can't', 'It's impossible', 'I'm so clumsy, so stupid', far too frequently. This is negative self-hypnosis, a process of putting unhelpful labels on yourself. Lift yourself up rather than put yourself down by dwelling on victories rather than on failures. Choose that which makes you feel good, praise yourself for your achievements.

If there is such a thing as the secret of life, perhaps it is to identify what it is you enjoy doing most, and do it as often as you can, preferably without inflicting too much pain on those around you. But at least go positively after these things that make you feel good rather than staying with those that make you feel bad.

Look for 'strokes', positive comments which are aimed in your direction. Most of us accept negative statements about ourselves without question, yet often find it difficult to accept compliments gracefully. Notice when someone remembers your name. That is a 'stroke'. The other person feels you are important enough for him or her to make the effort of memory. Enjoy phone calls from friends and acquaintances. They care enough to take the time to call you.

So many nice things happen which we overlook. Be friendly to yourself by bringing them to your attention. Perhaps a stray dog follows you home. Well, that's not something that happens to everyone. It shows how much good sense the dog has, to choose you rather than someone else. Enjoy the sunset, the feel of the breeze on your cheek, the smell of vegetation after rain. Also, learn how to become a winner of the Inner Game.

THE INNER GAME

In his book, *The Inner Game of Tennis*, Tim Gallwey applies Zen Buddhism to the playing of tennis, which he then uses as an example of playing the game of life itself. In tennis, Gallwey says, there are two games. The Outer Game is the obvious one. It involves the score on the board, the satisfaction of saying: 'I really hammered George today', and the trophies won.

However, Gallwey feels that the Inner Game is far more important. This is our contest against the obstacles we set up in our own minds, obstacles which prevent us from playing up to our capabilities. They include fear, lack of self-confidence, self-condemnation, trying too hard, lack of will to win, perfectionism, self-consciousness, frustration, anger, boredom, expectations and a busy mind. These obstacles tend to prevent us focusing all our energies on the task at hand, namely, playing tennis. In particular, they interfere with our concentration, which is one of the main skills of the Inner Game.

SKILLS OF THE INNER GAME

Gallwey sees **concentration** in terms of mental stillness. While the mind is busy with thoughts unrelated to the game, it cannot stay focused. Thus, Gallwey suggests we must put the mind somewhere in order to still it. One of his solutions is to watch the design on the tennis ball as it comes towards us, to concentrate so completely on this that we do not think of anything else.

Concentration, then, is the art of focusing our attention. It involves keeping our minds completely in the 'here and now', no easy task as any one who has attempted to follow his advice will attest. However, his view does coincide neatly with the ideas expressed in the previous chapter on the power of the mantra. This technique is effective in calming the mind because it provides a point of concentration. While we are focused on the repetition of the mantra, our thoughts do not veer off in other directions. The same effect is achieved by giving our undivided attention to our breathing, or to an external object such as a candle, or to an internal image such as miror-still lake.

Concentration is a vital skill of the Inner Game whether we are playing tennis or playing the game of life. In life, the Outer Game involves our salary, prestige, the size of our home, the opulence of our car, and the other trappings of wealth, whereas the Inner Game is the struggle against the self-defeating obstacles we create within our mind. The ability to calm our mind through concentration is of incalculable value in this struggle. So, too, are the other skills Gallwey discusses.

Letting go of the habit of judging is one of these. When we judge, we add an evaluation to an otherwise neutral event. In tennis, we may hit a backhand drive which goes out over the baseline. That is the neutral event, the ball going out. To this, it is easy to add the evaluation 'Blast, another bad backhand. I've got a hopeless backhand. I can never hit it in.' Based on this negative judgement, it is not too great a step to 'I'm a woeful tennis player' and even to 'I make a mess of everything I do. I'm just no good at things.'

This gross generalization then becomes a self-fulfilling prophecy expressed thus: 'Because I am not good at things, I will make a mess of whatever I do.' If the expectation of failure is present, the chances are quite strong that we will indeed make a mess of whatever we are doing. We tend to get what we expect and, in this tennis example, the negative self-evaluation all stems from one backhand drive which went out of court.

In the same way, we might blame ourselves for failing to close a business deal. If we do this several times, we can easily start telling ourselves we are inadequate. Keep this up and soon we believe in what we are telling ourselves, accepting the self-imposed evaluation that we are inadequate. Accordingly, we act in ways which are likely to lead to failure and confirm our negative evaluation.

Many, many people in all walks of life think like this. They take basically neutral events then impose upon them an evaluation which leads to a negative self-image and negative behaviour. To counter this tendency, let go of the habit of judgment. Allow things to be as they are without adding to them. The backhand drive lands out over the baseline. The business deal close was unsuccessful. That is all. Leave it like that. Observe in a detached way what happened, attempt to correct the error, then perform the action again. Continue to observe and modify, but leave the blaming out of it.

Through adoption of such an attitude, you can more easily motivate yourself to overcome the errors. Blame and negative evaluation are the enemies of effective self-motivation. They sap our desire to improve. Instead we wallow in self-pity over our inadequacy, fearing fresh challenges because they are likely to further reveal our incapacity.

Yet, learning to **welcome obstacles** is another skill of the Inner Game. As Gallwey puts it, we should love our opponent because he provides us with the opportunity to learn of our capabilities. The better he is, the more he pushes us, the deeper we dip into our own resources. In the business world the obstacles we meet challenge us to lift our performance, to develop our potential.

Welcome obstacles as friends for they provide the fuel for self-motivation. Accept life's unpleasant events as exercises, as challenges, for they stimulate us to climb previously unscaled heights. Still, we should be careful not to overdo it, to try too hard. In tennis, as in all sports, when we try too hard we tense our muscles to such an extent that we can no longer smoothly perform the actions necessary for success. In business, and in life generally, when we strive too hard we frequently get in our own way and that brings us to the final skill of the Inner Game.

This is a basic principle of Zen Buddhism, to **let it all happen** instead of trying to make it happen. Many practictioners of this philosophy believe that, for example, Westerners try so hard to find happiness that they let it slip through their fingers. To some extent this is true, yet, if all we do is wait for the things we want, we often never achieve our goals.

As in most things, a reasonable compromise is necessary. Doing nothing is likely to be as unproductive as striving too hard. If, by trying really hard, you are not achieving your objectives, ease off somewhat, stop pressing, and see if that improves the situation. Should you be letting it all happen yet accomplishing nothing, start doing things aimed at achieving what you want and observe the results. Just observe. Don't blame or criticize yourself. Note what occurs. Again, being your own expert is the only way to monitor your behaviour and learn what works best for you. When you do become aware of how you seem to operate best, then programme yourself to behave in this way more consistently.

UNCONSCIOUS PROGRAMMING

Though willpower may be the way to programme our conscious minds, imagination is likely to be more effective in stimulating change in the unconscious, that part of our mind which appears to control most aspects of our lives . Yet, we often use our imagination destructively.

Denise Ryder, an editor for a publishing company, always imagines the worst. If she is to take a trip, particularly if it involves flying, she will agonize for weeks beforehand, often worrying herself into a state of extreme distress. Yet, invariably, the actual trips are concluded quite successfully. None of the dreadful things which she imagines actually happens.

Similarly, she imagines dire outcomes for herself resulting from meetings at work, social engagements, and personal relationships. Imagination certainly rules Denise's life, but it is the rule of fear. If she would but substitute desire for fear, her imagination could become a powerful self-motivational weapon contributing to increased success in her life.

Apparently, the unconscious part of our mind cannot distinguish between that which we imagine and actual reality. This provides the basis for much of my therapy as I guide patients into imagining themselves as they want to be. Part of the success imagery I used with Denise involved her taking, in imagination, a flight the way she would like it to be rather than the way she feared it would be. From leaving home to arrival at her destination, this flight was relaxed, enjoyable, interesting.

Using the techniques I have discussed in *The Fantasy Factor*, I taught Denise how to distort time so that one hour on the clock would pass as if it was only five minutes. The flight thus seemed to be over very quickly. By mentally rehearsing this successful trip many times before it actually eventuated, Denise was able to overcome her normal pre-flight fears. This process is really one of making your own mental movies. To do so effectively, the following guidelines may be of use.

MAKING YOUR MENTAL MOVIES

- **Relaxation**
  Allow yourself to relax before creating your mental movies as this seems to improve the visualization process.

- **Make them real**

  Make your imagery detailed and specific, as close to the real thing as possible. Begin with something familiar in the situation, then add details until you have a sense of being there. 'See' yourself going through the real step-by-step sequence of actions.

- **Your own role in the movie**

  (i) Play the observer, 'watching' yourself perform— this is appropriate for reviewing a past experience or when you are using an ideal model.

  (ii) Play the participant, 'feeling' yourself perform— this is particularly useful for rehearsing a future event.

  To get the greatest value play both roles, initially 'seeing' how it looks from the outside as the observer, then 'feeling' and practising it from the inside as a participant.

- **Experience it fully**

  Employ as many of your senses as possible. 'See' the situation in your mind, 'hear' what is happening, 'feel' yourself in action, perhaps 'smell' and 'taste' something which is present. Some people can experience all five of these. Others may experience only one or two, yet they still are able to create successful movies.

- **Use a trigger**

  Select some action in your movie (tapping your foot, holding your hands in a certain way, touching your ring) which can be transfered to the real situation. Use this trigger physically as you visualize your movie.

In her movie, Denise substituted images of what she desired for images of what she feared. When she did so, she changed her attitude towards flying. In the same way, sportsmen and women have been able to improve their performance, salesmen and women to sell more successfully, managers to improve their employee relationships, and lovers to resurrect their moribund sexual relationships. We are what we think. If we send fear messages to the unconscious mind via our imaginations, we will be fearful. If we send success messages by imagining ourselves as we want to be, we will be successful. We can, in fact, use the fear images as cues to generate a success image. This is comparable to changing positives into negatives as outlined earlier.

Every time Denise imagines something fearful about an impending flight, she uses this as a signal to replace it immediately with a success image of herself handling the situation with pleasure. Every time a businessman finds himself anticipating another rejection, he switches to a success image of himself clinching the deal. It may not always produce the desired result but is far more likely to do so than continually feeding fear of failure messages into the unconscious mind.

In previous books, particularly *The Plus Factor*, I have emphasized the value of a technique known as **remaking the day**. Because so many businessmen and women have found it useful, I feel it is worthy of repetition here. It is particularly rewarding when done on your return home at the end of the day and before immersing yourself in family activities. Take about 10 minutes to get away quietly by yourself, relax a little, and go back over your day.

One at a time, mentally re-create things that have gone well for you. Relive them in your imagination, a number of times, congratulating yourself on these successes. Then, turn to the things that have not gone well for you. One at a time, wipe them from your mind and imagine yourself redoing them the way you would have preferred. Do this rerun about five or six times.

Because your mind does not distinquish between this imaginative reworking of your experience and the actual event, you may have mishandled it once, but now you are doing it correctly six times. The success outweighs the failure six to one and, if you make a regular practice of remaking your day so that it is perfect, you will find that gradually your days become better and better. You are programming your mind for success and wiping away the failures.

People who have not tapped into the power of this very simple technique dismiss it as useless daydreaming. However, many successful people have no compunction about acknowledging that they frequently daydream as a means of inspiring them to achieve particular goals. In other words, they use daydreams as a form of self-motivation. Remaking the day is just that, a way of guiding your imagination towards the objectives you see as desirable.

Michael Korda, in *Success*, puts it well when he says:

Allow yourself time for daydreaming, cultivate your daydreams, enjoy them. Above all, make them creative by linking them to your goal. . . . We would go to bed with hardly anyone if we weren't spurred on by our sexual fantasies. And the people we do go to bed with tend to satisy our sexual needs in direct proportion to the extent with which they coincide with our fantasies. Much the same is true of work. We work best, and most productively, when we are putting our fantasies into practice. Let yourself go, free your imagination, indulge your fantasies. . . . The more you can dream, the more you can do.

Good advice indeed. Through my work with businesspeople, sporting teams, students and patients seeking therapy, I have become convinced that the key to success is to **imagine yourself as you want to be and to then act as if you are already that person**. Last thing at night, as you drift off to sleep, feed positive images into your mind. 'See' yourself behaving as you want to behave, achieving the success you want to achieve. You'll find your dreams are very pleasant, your sleep deep and undisturbed, and you'll wake in the morning feeling good.

Remember as you wake that you have been given a

marvellous gift. You have been given a new day, a new life, one which you can use as you will. Bertrand Russell encapsulated much wisdom in a few words when he said: 'Every day is a new life to a wise man.' Start fresh each day determining to be the person you want to be. Use your imagination to help you as did Bill Glover.

When he first came to see me, Bill had just been promoted to head a Public Service department. Though he really wanted the position, he had doubts about his ability to do the job, this showing up as great uneasiness whenever he had to conduct meetings with his staff. He felt he handled this situation so badly that the staff were not taking him seriously. To help him feel more self-confident, I had Bill imagine himself conducting a meeting the way he would like to, confidently, decisively, efficiently. I encouraged him to do this several times each day and as he drifted off to sleep at night. In addition, he was to begin each day as if he was the confident, self-assured person he was imagining himself to be. He was, in other words, to play a role, to pretend he was such a person.

The great thing about the imagination is that, once stimulated, it tends to provide its own solutions. When Bill saw me two weeks after our first session, he told me his problem had disappeared. What had happened was that, each morning, as soon as he awoke, Bill mentally went into a telephone booth and put on his superman outfit. With the powers of superman, he sailed through the day confidently, with complete self-assurance. After ten days, Bill said that this was no longer necessary. Because he had found he was able to handle the job, his confidence had increased to the extent that he no longer needed his superman role. Though it would be easy to think of Bill's solution as somewhat childish, for him it worked. He achieved what he wanted and that is the criterion we must use if we are to become successful.

Bill chose to use imagery as the vehicle for his success message to the unconscious. Others, particularly those who do not find it easy to create mental images, use positive suggestion to achieve the same end. Many of my patients repeat the litany: 'I am calm, relaxed, confident and happy', feeling that this inspires them to achieve the state of being which they desire. Positive suggestions can be as simple as this or more formalized as in the procedure below.

POSITIVE SUGGESTION

- Take a suggestion and write it ten or twenty times in succession on a piece of paper. Use your name, writing it in the first ('I am calm, relaxed, confident and happy'), second ('You, Bob, are calm, relaxed, confident and happy'), and third persons ('Bob is calm, relaxed, confident and happy').
- As you write the words really think about their meaning. Notice whether you feel any resistance, doubts, or negative thoughts about what you are writing. Whenever you do, turn over the paper, and on the back write out the negative thought, the reason why the suggestion can't be true (for example, 'There is no way this will work'). Then go back to writing the suggestion.
- When you finish, look at the back of the paper. If you have been honest, you will have listed the reasons why you are keeping yourself from getting what you want.
- Think of some suggestions you can use to counteract these negative fears or beliefs, writing them out unless you prefer to stick to the original suggestion. You may want to modify this, making it more accurate.
- Once or twice daily, write out the suggestions. After a few days you can drop the ones relating to the negative programming and just keep writing the original suggestion.

One particular form of positive suggestion involves saying silently to yourself: 'I now call forth the quality

---

of 'strength' (or
Simply make a str
this quality is now co
can invoke the spirit o
qualities you admire.

Imagery and positive sugges
to generate the self-motivation
going. However, though motivat
energy for your success engine, it does
a sense of direction. In the next chapt
some ways of achieving this self-direction.

'wisdom', 'serenity', 'assertiveness').'

ong, clear statement to yourself that
ming to you. In the same way, you
a particular person who has the

tion will 'lift' you, helping
you need to keep you
ion may provide the
not necessarily give
r we will look at

...s par-
...ponder or give much thought to
...s. Just do it 'off the top of your head'. Put the list away, and repeat the process at the same time during each of the next five weeks. Then take out your six lists and read them. You will be left with little doubt about what is important to you.

Reading the lists may simply confirm that the goals towards which you are striving reflect the things you want most. On the other hand, you may find that your goals need revision because they are not motivating you to move in the direction of fulfilling your needs. If you repeat this Quick List Technique every six months, you will become aware of how your needs change. You may also realize that you are doing things to move you towards goals which are no longer important to you. Once you are aware of this, you can then modify your goals to reflect this change in needs.

Another way of identifying your goals is to ask yourself three key questions.

---

1 What are my lifetime goals?
2 How would I like to spend the next three years of my life?
3 If I knew I would be dead in six months, how would I use the time till then?

Take each question in turn and, without thinking too deeply about it, write down every answer that comes into your mind. Then spend two minutes going through your list and deciding on the three most important answers in order of priority.

When you have done this for each question, you will have up to nine answers, three for each question. Consider these, and decide on the three most important, in order of priority. These are your key goals.

These first two methods, which are the ones I normally use in the workshops I run with businesspeople, are general in character. However, it is possible to be more precise, in that goals may be specified for particular areas of your life.

- Write down the following categories:
  - Work/career
  - Money
  - Relationships
  - Personal grwoth and education
  - Life style/possessions
  - Creative self-expression
  - Leisure/travel
- For each of these catagories, write down some things you would like to have, or change, or improve in the near future. Do this 'off the top of your head' without thinking too hard about it.
- To stretch your imagination further, list each of the seven catagories and write a description of the most ideal situation you could imagine for each of them.

- From these ideal scenes, make a list of ten to twelve most important goals for your life as you feel them to be right now.
  - Select from these the most important goals you would like to achieve within the next five years.
  - Repeat the process to arrive at five to six goals for the coming year. These should move you in the same direction as your five year goals.
  - Be even more precise. Write out goals for six months, one month, and one week from now, choosing three to four that are most important as sub-stations along the way to achieving your longer range targets.

This might seem somewhat elaborate, yet it takes relatively little time to chart a course of action. Most successful people set targets, for human beings seem to need a sense of purpose to be effective. For some, the targets may be long term only. However, most of us need to have these long-term goals broken down into monthly, weekly, and daily targets. By setting ourselves sub-goals in this way, we can achieve the sense of self-direction so essential to success. We are able to reward ourselves frequently for many small achievements, instead of having to wait until we attain a big success before we can experience that satisfaction.

Though unexpected eventualities may disrupt progress towards these goals, self-directed people take these in their stride, carrying on unruffled.

WHAT IS IMPORTANT?

If you are comfortable with the idea that the attainment of your goals defines success, it is important to ascertain that the goals you have choosen for yourself actually suit your personality. One way of checking on this is to answer the following questions. If you answer these questions honestly, you are likely to gain greater insight into your values and, by looking at these, you may become better acquainted with what is most meaningful for you.

YOUR VALUES AND ASPIRATIONS

1 Name the three people you admire most.
2 Name the three people you would most like to be.
3 List the three nicest things anyone has said about you.
4 Which was the happiest day of your life?
5 Which was the most miserable day of your life?
6 Name the person to whom you feel closest.
7 Of which accomplishment are you most proud?

Are your goals appropriate for the type of person you present in these answers?

After a couple of weeks, reread what you have written. Are your answers still the same?

Another way of achieving this insight is for you to imagine the following three situations and your responses to them.

- You need to escape from your present home and are permitted to take with you only ten of your current possessions. What would they be?
- At the moment of your death, what will be of most importance to you? What will it take by way of accomplishments, attitudes, or possessions for you to die satisfied?
- Write your own epitaph. In one sentence, say how you would like to be remembered.

SETTING GOALS FOR OTHERS

In this chapter, the emphasis so far has been upon the setting of goals for ourselves. Now, let us look at the situation when your responsibility is wider, when it becomes necessary to help others set and achieve goals. A person who is able to do this very successfully is Ken Foxley, the manager of an electronics firm.

Ken's approach embodies four 'basic principles of goal setting', the first of which is to **get agreement and commitment**. This involves consulting other people who are involved and keeping them informed. Although such a procedure seems commonsense, many managers do not follow it. Instead, after imposing their goals from above, they wonder why their salesmen and office staff don't show the enthusiasm they expect. If we are consulted and our opinions valued, we are more likely to commit ourselves to achieving the goals sought by management.

Ken believes this. Accordingly he consults his staff when he is defining a goal for the firm. This may be, for example, a particular sales target for the coming quarter. With his sales staff, he explores the possibilities to arrive at a reasonable figure. Together they work out an action plan likely to achieve this target and, as this is put into effect, further consultation takes place along the way to ensure continued commitment.

The second principle embodied in Ken's approach, that of **reducing goals to a manageable size**, is implicit in the previous one. It involves asking very specific questions in order to narrow a goal, questions such as 'How much?', 'How often?', 'Which precise product?'. The importance of asking such questions will be elaborated later in the chapter on communication. In the present context the purpose is to enable everyone involved in the achievment of the goal to visualize a realistic, tangible result.

Accordingly, the goal is to be **stated precisely**. This third principle, Ken feels, is where most people come to grief. They are too indefinite in the goal they set. He believes that it is necessary to specify measurable results, set target dates, and establish cost limitations. The general form of such a goal statement is:

> 'To (action or accomplishment verb) (single measureable result) by (target date) at (cost in money, hours of effort, or both).'

An example of how such a goal might look in practice would be:

> 'To (sell) (1000 stereo units) by (31 August) at (an average cost of £300 per unit).'

Once goals have been precisely defined, Ken, in collaboration with his sales staff, **sets up specific action plans** designed to effect their achievement. This is his fourth principle. They may decide upon a series of separate activities designed to achieve the goal, or to go through a sequence of progressive events building towards the climax of the 1000 sales. Often this involves setting a number of smaller, short-term goals. If, in the example above, 31 August was the end of the quarter, separate targets might be established for each of the three months with contingency plans to be put into action if these were not attained.

These four principles have served Ken well. Many readers may find them obvious. They are. Yet, just because they are obvious does not mean that they are put into practice. Many people simply do not behave in this way. The result is that if they do set goals, these are so vague that their realization is extremely unlikely. This was Ken's problem when he first began his business, but adoption of the four principles got him moving. He has never looked back.

Another way of getting moving is to consider the following questions.

- What programme/project/action do you most want to get moving on now?
- Who or what is the key to getting it moving?
- What obstacles must be overcome for it to work?
- What in your behaviour is likely to help or hinder its movement?

- What action will you take to increase your own effectiveness in getting it moving?
- What help do you need from others? How will you get this help?

The above questions are ones which it is well worth encouraging your staff to ask of themselves. While it is a common human trait to talk about doing things rather than to actually do them, these questions may stimulate your staff into setting goals for themselves, goals which they then put into action. In short, they are likely to become more effective, and successful, individuals.

In addition to their ability to set and achieve goals for themselves, effective individuals generally share a number of other important characteristics. These characteristics include taking effective decisions, making use of and building on the strengths of other people, reducing stress by developing an activity which acts as a positive addiction, concentrating on the few major areas where superior performance will produce outstanding results, focusing on results rather than activity, and managing time well.

Decision making and utilizing the strengths of others will be considered in the chapter on working with others, while stress reduction is the subject of the following chapter. However, the other characteristics may be included under the general heading of effective time management.

HOW DO YOU USE YOUR TIME?

Most of us have only the vaguest idea of how we actually spend our time. That is why a **Time Log** can be so useful. This involves keeping, for a week, a detailed diary of how you spend every minute of your day. It does take something of an effort to do this, even for as short a period as one week, but the benefits are well worth it. What you will probably find is that most of the value of your week, probably around 80 per cent, will come from relatively few, probably around 20 per cent, of your activities.

Successful people derive satisfaction from what they do, a satisfaction which stems from achievement of goals. When we attain something important to us, we feel good about it. Conversely, if we are spending time doing things which we think really don't matter to us, we are unlikely to feel any sense of fulfilment or satisfaction. If your Time Log shows that up to 80 per cent of the things you do are not particularly productive, you are unlikely to be living a successful life. You are devoting too much time to activities not moving you in the direction you want to go.

One of the keys to using your time in a way that is both productive and satisfying is to focus your attention on doing those tasks which, though not urgent, are important. When a task is both urgent and important, we don't have to think about whether we have time to do it or not. We do it. However, a trap into which it is easy to fall is to put off doing things which will move us towards our goals because of pressure exerted by other tasks. These tend to have a sense of urgency about them, even though they might be quite trivial in nature.

Take a very simple example. Ken Foxley, referred to earlier, loves woodworking. It is his only hobby. Let's assume that at the moment he is making an ornamental chest. Though a very time consuming job, this is a labour of love for Ken and he is, on this particular day, really looking forward to spending several hours in his workshop during the evening. This is important to him because, not only is his hobby a source of relaxation from his business activities, it also provides the satisfaction of creative achievement which is one of his strongest personal goals.

Late in the afternoon, a neighbour drops in to ask Ken and his wife to come over that evening to look at photographs taken during a recent holiday. Ken remembers similar boring evenings, spent with people in whom he has little interest. Yet, here is his well-meaning neighbour standing in front of him with this invitation.

Under these conditions, many people, usually out of politeness, accept the invitation, sacrificing time which could have been spent in doing something of value to them. They do so because, though the activity suggested is trivial and of no important to them, a person is standing there in front of them waiting for an answer and thus creating a certain sense of pressure or urgency. Of course, the usual outcome is that, over the course of the entire evening, the person who has reluctantly accepted the invitation, silently curses himself for not saying 'No'.

Ken, however, has adopted one of the principles outlined in an earlier chapter, that of being selfish. Gracefully he refuses the invitation, and by so doing, ensures that the evening will provide for him a sense of satisfaction instead of a feeling of frustration. He can behave in this way because he knows what is important to him and what is not. At times we all have to make concessions in that we cannot always do what seems to be of most value to us. However, we usually limit ourselves in this regard far more than we need to.

So the essence of using time well is to know what we want. Unless we are clear on our goals, we can easily confuse activity with achievement. A successful person is not satisfied with a lot of busy work which, though it may fill in time and look impressive, is not getting him where he wants to be. It is the results he is producing that count, not how many hours he is putting in to attain those results. By concentrating his energy on a few major areas where superior performance will produce outstanding results, he is able to accomplish a great deal in relatively little time. Instead of dissipating his efforts, he focuses them where they will do the most good. That is the secret of successful time management.

This is why the Time Log is so useful. It shows us not only how we are allocating our time but also indicates how we tend to waste time, usually in the same way and with the same people. A **Time-wasted Log**, kept for just one week, will make this even clearer.

TIME-WASTER'S LOG

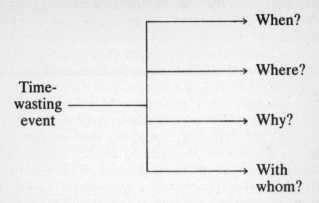

TIME AND ENERGY

Wasting time consumes a lot of energy. When we have no sense of accomplishment, work seems dreary and uninteresting. So, to generate energy, set things up so that you give yourself this sense of getting things done. One of the best ways of doing so is to **divide your day into small segments** of time, each one of which is treated as independent and valuable in itself. By structuring your day in this way you can get started on one task, complete it, experience a sense of achievement, then move on to the next one.

In *Man's Search for Meaning*, Viktor Frankl argues that there is no meaning in life other than that which we put into it ourselves. In his therapeutic system, Logotherapy, he suggests that each day we set up challenges for ourselves, small though they may be, so that we gain a sense of satisfaction from meeting and overcoming them. By dividing our day into many small time segments, each with its own task, that is what we are actually doing. As we cross each task off our list, we gain a sense of achievement, a feeling of making progress.

In fact, **making lists and setting priorities** is the basis of all effective time management. A television producer of my acquaintance, June Ramsey, makes this her last action before leaving her office each evening. She takes a few moments to note down the things she wants to do next day, listing them in order of importance. Though she expects interruptions which will take her away from these items, she knows she will always have her number one priority as a focus of attention until it is completed. With this crossed off her list, she concentrates her energy on the number two item.

When I first met June, she was having trouble in keeping up with her workload, something that had never happened to her before. She seemed unable to concentrate her energy on doing the things which had to be done, dissipating it in all sorts of trivial ways instead. To assist her solve this problem, I encouraged her to use the **Premack Principle**.

It has been said that to develop energy, it helps to treat yourself like a child. In a way that is what the Premack Principle does—it has sometimes been called 'Grandma's remedy' or 'You don't get to eat your dessert until you have eaten your vegetables'. That is, if there are two tasks involved, always do the least enjoyable one first, then reward yourself by doing the second one.

In June's case, the daily tasks she enjoyed most were opening her mail, making telephone calls, and talking over the production schedule with her assistants. She also derived considerable pleasure from coffee breaks and social chit-chat with friends who worked in other offices in the building.

To get June working efficiently again was simply a matter of using these enjoyable activities as rewards for doing ones which were not so enjoyable. Before she could open her mail, June had to spend an hour preparing a written production schedule, something she usually put off for as long as possible because she saw it as her most unpleasant task for the day. In fact, should there be something you find really unpleasant, do it first thing if you possibly can. Otherwise, it builds up stress within you because you know you have to do it some time. The longer you put it off, the harder it gets and the more pressure on you it exerts. Once you have done it, reward yourself.

June chose attending to her mail as her reward. Once she completed this, she embarked on another of her not-so-enjoyable tasks. This had to be finished before she could take a coffee break with one of her friends. Restructuring her day in this way enabled June to handle her workload without difficulty and, as a pleasant bonus, she found she had far more energy.

Her assistant, Alan Hargreaves, also mobilized his energy effectively, but made use of a somewhat different approach. One of the most common obstacles to working energetically is leaving tasks unfinished. Although some people are able to cope with incompleteness, they are a relatively small minority to which Alan did not belong. When he set out to do something he liked to complete it. If he was unable to do so, he found his enthusiasm waning. This is because energy seems to thrive on achievement and as things drag on repetitiously, it declines rapidly.

So Alan, whenever possible, would not start a task if he didn't think he could complete it within the time he had available. He would begin his day with a relatively simple job which could be finalized quickly, thus providing an immediate sense of achievement. From this he would progress to something a little more difficult, and then gradually move up to the really tough problems. In this way, Alan was working from a position of strength, having already achieved something in the day. However, should he have begun with a difficult and very time consuming task, something with which he was really struggling, then it is likely his energy would have quickly ebbed away.

Alan's approach is one I advocate for students taking examinations. I advise them to always begin with the easiest question first, then move on to the next easiest, and finish with the most difficult. Often, as students answers one question, they get ideas about later questions. If they stop and jot down these ideas as they come, later questions become much easier than they first seemed.

It's a matter of personality really. With Alan, each successfully completed task raised his confidence level, increasing his energy and enthusiasm. June, however, found the Premack Principle suited her better. Disposing of her most unpleasant and difficult task first was a great relief, one that charged her up for the rest of the day. Also, Alan's approach has the inbuilt difficulty that some tasks cannot be completed at one burst. That is where the '**Swiss Cheese method**' comes in.

When you have a big project, nibble away at the edges, poke holes in it. Should you have ten minutes clear, tell yourself you'll do something very small, maybe just writing a couple of paragraphs. Probably you'll become interested and actually spend more than the ten minutes on it. If you make a practice of doing this, you'll find that when you get the time clear to really tackle this big project, you have already done most of the work required. If you haven't already used this approach, try it. You will be very pleasantly surprised.

I have applied it very successful to writing books. Although it is tempting to wait until a block of uncommitted time appears before I start writing, I use odd moments to write a few sentences here, a couple of paragraphs there. In fact, when I have to stop writing, I deliberately do so in the middle of a sentence. It is far easier to resume writing when you have to finish a sentence than it is to begin a new section. Should I complete a chapter, I don't stop there but continue on to write a few sentences into the next chapter. Working in that way would probably drive Alan mad, but it suits me. As I said previously, it is a matter of personality so try out these approaches to find the one that seems to suit you, the one that keeps your energy flowing best.

HOW EXECUTIVES STAY ENERGETIC

It is no easy thing to keep your energy level high. The day-to-day work of executives, for example, is largely a matter of dealing with other people's needs and problems. They are constantly giving out, motivating and energizing others, but often giving little thought as to how they can motivate and re-energize themselves. The methods discussed above and in the previous chapter may help. So too may the following ideas, gathered from interviews with successful executives and reported by Jane Bensahel in the journal, *Personal Development*.

The head of a utility company put it this way: 'I force myself into a situation in which I have to sell. It could be presenting a new idea to my board, or trying to shake a subordinate out of a rut, or planning a speech. Whatever the specific outlet, the point is that by trying to stimulate others' enthusiasm, I can't help but get caught up in my own arguments.'

Energy may be generated, too, by taking an enthusiastic subordinate out to lunch. He or she usually has a number of exciting things on the go and, as he or she talks about these, the feeling of enthusiasm is contagious. Another executive commented: 'I make a list of reasons why I'm doing this to myself'. On those occasions when he felt 'down', this man needed to remind himself of the larger goals towards which he was working, goals which went beyond the day-to-day headaches.

Other executives took a day off when they were over-involved and emotionally drained by their work. It didn't seem to matter what they did on this day as long as it had nothing whatsoever to do with work. Actually, when it is impossible to physically remove yourself from your office to do this, a substitute is to take a mental holiday each day, an idea explored fully in *The Fantasy Factor*. What it involves is to take a ten to twenty minute break in which you 'turn-off' the world and go into a peaceful little world of your own creation. This may involve simply thinking of yourself in very positive ways, remembering a previous happy time, going to a special place, or looking forward to a future holiday.

Holidays can hold a special sort of magic, even if you don't actually leave the office. One of the executives interviewed by Bensahel told her he regenerated himself by pretending he was going on holiday the following week. As he said: 'You know how right before you're about to go away you get that "this-is-it" burst of energy to clear up all sorts of things? Once or twice, when I did this, it was so effective that the following week I really did have very little left to do.'

Actually, the most frequently mentioned approach was discussed in some detail earlier, that of focusing on an immediate goal and pursuing it through to completion. As one man put it: 'I find some aspect of a project that I particularly like to do and go ahead and do it to completion. I make it my top priority, no matter what else comes up, for a limited period of time. In this way I lift my spirits through the completion of something I really enjoy.'

This concept of focusing intensely on one thing at a time is vital to successful time management. Taken to its logical conclusion, it means that you **clear everything off your desk except the one task** on which you are presently engaged. If other material is left on your desk, your concentration is likely to be adversely affected. Out of the corner of your eye you see something that may require attention later. This starts you thinking about it, and your attention is distracted.

Put such material away in a drawer. In fact, its a good idea to have several drawers, one for your high priority tasks which must be done, one for tasks of moderate priority, and one for those things which may not require any action at all. Fortunately, quite a lot of the material we receive falls into this latter catagory. Making use of a simple perpetual filing system may help you identify such material.

PERPETUAL FILING SYSTEM

- 43 manila folders are required.
  - –Number 31 of these from 1 to 31 to accommodate the days of the month.
  - –Number 12 of these from 1 to 12 to accommodate the months of the year.
- Incoming material is filed under a day of the present month or a day of a future month.
- Each morning take out the file for that day, sorting material into the appropriate drawer, high, medium, or low priority.
- First day of each month, take out the folder for that month and sort the material into the 31 daily folders.

  For each document in the file, ask yourself 'What is the worst thing that could happen if this did not exist?' If the consequences are minimal, discard the document.

This approach is simplicity itself but does help you sort out those things about which you really do not need to bother.

Returning to the concept of tackling only one thing at a time, once you finish the task of the moment, remove that completely from your desk. Then take out whatever is necessary for handling the next item on your priority list.

Before leaving work in the evening, prepare your desk for the morning by placing on it only material pertinent to the one task which is to begin your day. In this way, you save a great deal of time when you arrive at work. I know of many business people who, when they enter their offices in the morning, waste a lot of time deciding what to do first. If you have already made that decision before you left work the previous day, you enter your office and there, awaiting you, is the initial task. It is then quite easy to make an immediate start.

In addition to this focusing of attention on a single task, two main points emerged from what these men and women were saying. The first is that you need to identify what gets you down and do something different. If, for example, many diverse, simultaneous demands from others upset you, give yourself a 'quiet hour' when you isolate yourself from others and set your own pace and direction.

The second is to identify what makes you feel good. When your energy is low, indulge yourself by doing one of these things. In fact, by deliberately seeking pleasures as part of each work day, you are likely to greatly reduce the number of times you feel a lack of energy.

It is useful, too, to put into practice the principle, expressed in the previous chapter on self-motivation, of acting as if you are the person you want to be. Most successful people convey a feeling of energy by walking at a fast, purposeful pace—so move decisively. Nor do they slouch, hands in pockets, stomach sticking out. Rather their bodies convey a sense of energy with an erect stance, squared shoulders, head up and stomach in. Your body, too, can transmit such a message.

Perhaps, like many successful people, you can become used to carrying a folder. This not only conveys purposefulness, but is also a convenient way of keeping hands out of pockets. Whether the folder actually contains anything of importance or not is irrelevant. It is the sense of 'doing something' engendered by this simple action that is the relevant factor. If we act as if we are energetic and successful, not only will we feel it ourselves but others will tend to accept us at our own valuation. The image we create goes a long way, becoming a self-fulfiling prophecy.

There are, also, quite specific exercises available to generate energy. Because some of the best of these are derived from Yoga, which has its origins in a culture different from our own, many Western business people look upon them as somewhat weird. That is unfortunate for they can often transform lethargy into energy very quickly. Perhaps you might like to try the following one, reserving judgement on whether it is likely to be useful or not until you have practised it a few times and observed its effects.

ENERGIZING YOURSELF

- Lie down on your back, eyes closed, arms at your sides or with hands clasped on your stomach. Breathe gently, deeply, and allow yourself to relax.
- Imagine a glowing sphere of golden light surrounding your head. Focus your attention on this sphere and, as you slowly and deeply breathe in and out five times, feel it radiate out from the top of your head as the energy expands.
- Repeat this procedure as, in turn, you imagine a golden sphere of light emanating from:
  - —your throat;
  - —the centre of your chest;
  - —your solar plexus;
  - —your pelvic area;
  - —your feet.

  In each case, breathe into the golden sphere five times, feeling the light energy radiating and expanding.
- Now imagine all the spheres of light glowing at once so that your body is radiating energy from the six points like a strand of jewels.
- Breathe deeply. As you breathe out, imagine energy flowing down along the left side of your body from the top of your head to your feet. As you breathe in, imagine it flowing up the right side of your body to your head. Repeat this circulation pattern three times.
- Continuing to breathe deeply, visualize, as you slowly exhale, the flow of energy going from the top of your head down along the front of your body to your feet. As you inhale, feel it flow up along the back of your body to the top of your head. Repeat this circulation three times.

- Finally, imagine the energy gathering at your feet from where it flows slowly up through the centre of your body to your head. From the top of your head it radiates out like a fountain of light and then flows back down the outside of your body to your feet. Repeat several times, or as often as you wish.

This exercise helps you increase your energy. However, there are occasions when it it necessary to deliberately reduce your arousal, calming yourself in order to handle stress more successfully.

7 Managing Stress

AROUSAL AND THE C ZONE

For some years it has been known that there exists a
link between level of stress (defined as arousal) and performance. If the stress level is too high or too low, performance is poor, whereas if we are operating at optimum
arousal we perform really well. Knowing that this is so
is one thing. Being able to identify our optimum arousal
level is another, for it is a very individual thing. However
a recent book, *The C Zone: Peak Performance Under
Pressure*, written by Robert and Marilyn Kriegel, indicates one way this identification might be achieved.

According to the Kriegels, when we are in the C Zone,
work is a delight. We are operating at our best, moving
back and forth between the challenge of learning new
things and the mastery of doing things we already know
how to do.

Challenge and mastery are the two key concepts of C
Zone theory. When we move out of our C Zones, it is
because of we have lost the balance between these two
elements. If we take on too much challenge, too much
that is new at the expense of having sufficient mastery in
our lives, we go into the Panic Zone. There we feel over-
pressured. As the Kriegels put it, people in this zone are
ruled by 'I gotta; I gotta do this; I gotta do that'. They
experience too much stress.

On the other hand, if we spend so much time doing the
things over which we already have a sense of mastery,

leaving little time for the challenge of the new, we go into the Drone Zone. Here the ruling words are 'I can't'. We're afraid to take any sort of risk, make any change. It's all too frightening. In this zone, there is a lack of the stress necessary to motivate action.

The Kriegels diagram their zonal concept as shown below.

If you would like to know the zone in which you normally operate, the Performance Zone Profile, which I have adapted from *The C Zone*, will give you a reasonably accurate estimate.

On a piece of paper, set up six columns: Panic, Drone, C, CM, CF, CT. These last three represent the Type C characteristics: commitment (CM), confidence (CF), and control (CT).

Now compare your answers from the test with those on the score sheet which indicates the point value and performance zone for each possible answer (that is, a score of 2C = 2 points in the C column). If your score on a particular question falls in the Panic (P) or Drone (D) category, simply add the point score to that column.

If you score in the C Zone, give yourself the indicated number of points in the C column. Additionally when you score a C, look at column no. 8 on the score sheet to determine the Type C characteristic being tested by that question. (Some questions have only one characteristic, others two.) Then enter the number of C points you received for that answer into appropriate Type C characteristic column. You get CM, CF or CT points only when you have a C score.

For example, in scoring question 1, if your answer was a 3, give yourself 1 point in the Drone column. However, if your answer was a 5, give yourself 2 points in the C column and 2 points in both the CF and CT columns.

Compare your total scores in the first three columns: Panic, Drone and C. Your score will be highest in the zone you occupy the most often. This will give you an indication of how you tend to stray away from your C zone. A Type C person generally scores twice as many C points as Drone and Panic points combined.

The CM, CF, and CT columns will indicate which Type C characteristics are well developed and which need work. If your strength, in terms of these characteristics, far outweighs your weak points, you may be relying too much on that characteristic and too little on the others. A perfect Type C would score 30 points in each catagory, but then, who's perfect?

PERFORMANCE ZONE PROFILE

Answer each question honestly by circling the number which most accurately describes your behaviour as it actually is, not as you would like it to be or how you think it should be.. If you completely agree with a statement, circle number 7; if you completely disagree, circle number 1. If your agreement or disagreement is less complete, circle an appropriate number between these two extremes.

1 I can do anything I try.	1 2 3 4 5 6 7
2 I am constantly in over my head.	1 2 3 4 5 6 7
3 I'll try anything once.	1 2 3 4 5 6 7
4 I am an overachiever.	1 2 3 4 5 6 7
5 I'm unwilling to try something about which I am unsure.	1 2 3 4 5 6 7
6 I often become so involved I lose track of time.	1 2 3 4 5 6 7
7 I'll do anything to achieve my goals.	1 2 3 4 5 6 7
8 I seek challenges.	1 2 3 4 5 6 7
9 I find it difficult to pull out when I fail.	1 2 3 4 5 6 7
10 I accept new ideas very cautiously.	1 2 3 4 5 6 7
11 My work is my life.	1 2 3 4 5 6 7
12 I am a stickler for details.	1 2 3 4 5 6 7
13 I play it safe.	1 2 3 4 5 6 7
14 I feel I have to constantly prove myself.	1 2 3 4 5 6 7
15 I want to be the best at what I do.	1 2 3 4 5 6 7
16 I'd rather be safe than sorry.	1 2 3 4 5 6 7
17 I don't prepare fully enough for important events.	1 2 3 4 5 6 7

18 I drive myself hard.	1 2 3 4 5 6 7
19 I have a dream for which I aim.	1 2 3 4 5 6 7
20 I set my goals higher than I can reach.	1 2 3 4 5 6 7
21 I bite off more than I can chew.	1 2 3 4 5 6 7
22 I am an eternal optimist.	1 2 3 4 5 6 7
23 I don't like to take chances.	1 2 3 4 5 6 7
24 Before I act, I think things through thoroughly.	1 2 3 4 5 6 7
25 If I fail something really important, life is not worth living.	1 2 3 4 5 6 7
26 I feel I am always rushing.	1 2 3 4 5 6 7
27 I never give up.	1 2 3 4 5 6 7
28 I must do well.	1 2 3 4 5 6 7
29 I push myself to the limit.	1 2 3 4 5 6 7
30 My commitments leave me little time to relax.	1 2 3 4 5 6 7
31 I get 'high' from my work.	1 2 3 4 5 6 7
32 I play by the rules.	1 2 3 4 5 6 7
33 Before I act, I carefully consider every possibility.	1 2 3 4 5 6 7
34 There is virtually nothing I can't do.	1 2 3 4 5 6 7
35 Before I finish one job, I move on to the next one.	1 2 3 4 5 6 7

ACHIEVING OPTIMUM PERFORMANCE

This C Zone concept developed by the Kriegels is a very useful way of looking at the way we function. If we spend most of our time in the C Zone, we have achieved an optimum performance level. This is usually characterized by:

- the establishment and updating of goals;
- concentration on high rather than low priority items;
- the practice of effective time management;
- knowledge of stress points;
- practising the 'good health habits'.

PERFORMANCE ZONE PROFILE

Score Sheet

	1	2	3	4	5	6	7	8
1	2D	2D	1D	2C	2C	1P	3P	CF/CT
2	2D	1D	1C	2C	1P	2P	3P	CM/CT
3	2D	2D	1D	2C	2C	1P	3P	CF
4	3D	2D	1D	—	2C	1P	3P	CM
5	2P	2C	2C	1D	2D	3D	3D	CF/CT
6	3D	3D	2D	1D	2C	1C	2P	CM
7	3D	2D	1D	1C	2C	1P	2P	CM
8	3D	2D	1D	1D	2C	2C	2P	CF/CT
9	—	2C	1C	—	—	—	—	CF
10	2P	1P	2C	1C	1D	2D	3D	CF
11	3D	2D	1D	1C	2C	1P	3P	CM
12	3P	2P	1P	2C	1C	—	1D	CT
13	2P	1C	2C	—	1D	2D	3D	CF/CT
14	—	—	1C	2C	—	—	*	CF
15	3D	3D	2D	1D	2C	1C	1P	CM
16	3P	1P	2C	—	1D	2D	3D	CF/CT
17	1D	2C	1C	1P	2P	3P	3P	CT/CM
18	3D	2D	1D	—	2C	1P	2P	CM
19	2D	2D	2D	1D	1C	2C	1P	CM
20	3D	2D	1D	—	2C	1P	3P	CM
21	3D	2D	1D	1C	2C	1P	3P	CM
22	3D	2D	1D	1C	2C	1C	2P	CF
23	2P	2C	2C	1D	2D	3D	3D	CF/CT
24	3P	3P	2P	1P	2C	—	1D	CT
25	1C	2C	1C	—	—	—	—	CF
26	2D	1D	1C	2C	1P	2P	3P	CT
27	3D	2D	1D	1C	2C	1P	3P	CM
28	—	—	1C	2C	—	—	—	CF
29	3D	3D	2D	1D	2C	1P	3P	CM
30	3D	2D	1D	1C	2C	1P	3P	CM/CT
31	3D	3D	2D	1D	—	2C	2C	CM
32	2P	1C	2C	—	1D	2D	3D	CF/CT
33	3P	2P	1P	1C	2C	1D	2D	CT
34	3D	3D	2D	1D	2C	2C	2P	CF
35	—	1C	2C	—	—	—	—	CT

The first three of these have been covered in the previous chapter. As for the fourth one, this involves 'listening' to your body to identify the signals which indicate you are becoming over-stressed. For many people, this signal is fatigue or tenseness in the stomach. Others express their over-arousal through headaches or backaches. Though each of us does tend to experience stress differently, the way we do is usually the same on every occasion. Thus, we can use this physical signal as a warning.

It is a warning we should heed. Increasingly, medical evidence is linking stress with a wide range of serious illness including heart disease and cancer. It appears as if our bodies use physical symptoms to tell us that slowing down would be a good idea. If we ignore such warnings, the symptoms become progressively worse until we are forced to stop.

In *The Stress Factor*, I elaborated upon this stress-illness link in some detail. Expressed briefly, the key idea is that if your are showing a number of symptoms such as anxiety, irritability, poor concentration, inability to relax, headache, stomach upset, insomnia, ulcers, high blood pressure, withdrawal from relationships, increased smoking, increased alcohol consumption, and more frequent use of tranquillizers, the chances are that you need to look at your current life style in an effort to reduce the pressure you are experiencing.

You might also consider practising the 'good health habits' which are characteristic of many people who spend most of their time in the C Zone of optimum performance. It has been experimentally confirmed that those of us who practise all seven of these habits generally enjoy better health than those practising six, who in turn are healthier than those with five, and so on down the scale.

However, although this finding holds true when groups of people are compared, we must provide latitude for individual differences. When I first read of these health habits, I realized that whereas earlier in my life I seemed to need seven to eight hours of sleep a night to feel at my best, as I grew older, sleeping for six hours would be all I required to feel alert and energetic.

Similarly, there are some people who do not eat breakfast. They just don't like to. If, for some reason, they have something to eat first thing in the morning, they feel physically the worse for it. It would not seem wise, therefore, for such people to change their habit as long as they are feeling healthy.

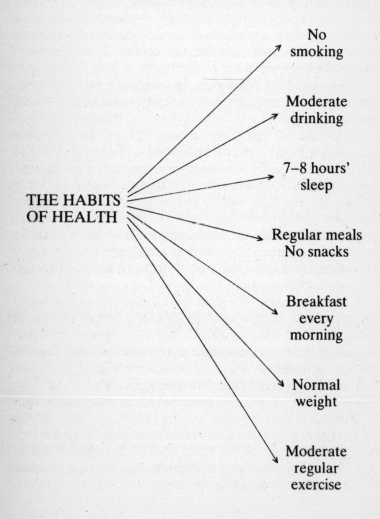

THE HABITS
OF HEALTH

No
smoking

Moderate
drinking

7–8 hours'
sleep

Regular meals
No snacks

Breakfast
every
morning

Normal
weight

Moderate
regular
exercise

Despite the proviso that individual differences do exist, these seven 'habits of health' do make a lot of sense, tending to summarize much research into the improvement of human health. By adopting them, you maximize your chances of feeling healthy and of performing at your optimum level of efficiency.

If your Performance Zone Profile placed you in this optimum level of efficiency area, the stress you experience would appear to be appropriate, providing sufficient stimulation to spur you to perform well without adversely affecting your health. You are probably experiencing, in fact, what Hans Selye, the doyen of stress researchers, has referred to as eustress.

This is the stress of winning, of meeting and overcoming challenges, and is in marked contrast to the negative attitude we usually take towards the word 'stress'. This negative aspect is distress, the stress of losing. It is distress which becomes paramount when we stray into the Panic and Drone Zones, when our arousal levels are too high or too low respectively.

AVOIDING OVER- AND UNDER-AROUSAL

Should we find that we score high in the Panic Zone, to improve our performance and to reduce distress, we need to avoid over-arousal or, as it is frequently called today, 'burn-out'. The key to achieving this lies in reducing our stimulation intake.

TO REDUCE OVER-AROUSAL

1 Give yourself private, uninterrupted time, free of other people.
2 Assert your rights by learning to say 'No'.
3 Find out in advance what stress is involved in your work.
4 Avoid the myth of indispensability by delegating responsibilities.
5 Break large projects into smaller tasks, each of which is handled separately.

People usually provide stimulation, so if you are in the Panic Zone you need to reduce inter-personal contacts in favour of more time spent quietly alone. This is one reason for learning to say 'No' gracefully. As pointed out earlier, we often do things we don't want to because we are reluctant to refuse. We want to be loved, or at least liked, by everyone and we fear that if we say 'No', we will displease others. Possibly we will. However, the truth is that no matter how pleasant we are, and no matter how many helpful things we do, someone will dislike us. Bending over backwards to be agreeable is likely to result in our becoming 'doormats'.

It has been said that the essence of tact is to be able to refuse a dinner invitation without giving a reason. This comment can be generalized to virtually all situations in which we want to say 'No'. Because of a commendable desire to avoid hurting the feelings of others, we usually support our refusal with an excuse, often one that is untrue. Unfortunately, the other person may then show that our excuse does not hold water, and therefore we really will be able to do whatever it is we have just refused.

To overcome this, it is possible to say something like: 'I'm sorry. I'm unable to do that,' and stop. It comes as a bit of a shock at first, and it is not easy to do in the face of our upbringing which encourages us to tell 'white lies' instead of being more honest. But it is quite surprising how quickly other people will accept your direct statement as long as you speak pleasantly and unaggressively. In fact, it is likely that you will be treated with more respect as you assert yourself quietly but firmly.

Learning in advance of likely work stress is a rather obvious way of reducing stimulation because the unexpected is always more arousing than events for which we have prepared. Helpful, too, is the practice of delegating responsibilies. Many Panic Zone people seem to feel that they must do everything and that, unless they do, all will crash in ruins about them.

An ex-patient of mine, Charles Mortimer, was very

much like that. Fortunately Charles possessed a sense of humour, something that is often lacking in people who feel indispensible. I was able to use this characteristic of his to overcome both his sleeping difficulties and, more generally, his normal state of over-arousal. All it took was to suggest to Charles that when he went to bed at night, he might let God run the world while he slept. He, Charles, could then take over when he woke up in the morning. More than all the earnest advice, this off-the-cuff comment helped him realize that his behaviour was making life difficult for himself and for those who worked with him. In fact, Charles was often able to let God run the world until lunchtime, at which time he though he had better take over again.

Charles also adopted the idea, suggested in the chapter on self-direction, that he sub-divide large projects, setting up a number of small targets instead of one large general goal. He found this took a lot of pressure off him.

Avoiding under-arousal, or 'rust-out', involves the opposites of the ideas discussed above. It is necessary to increase the input of stimulation. In my marital counselling, I have found that one of the main reasons for difficulties in a marriage is that husband and wife exist in different zones. Thus, when one partner of the marriage, who may be in the Drone Zone, seeks additional stimulation, the other, who may be in the Panic Zone, wants less. If they insist of doing everything together as a couple, it is inevitable that there will be conflict. When one is getting what he or she wants, the other is not. An approach more likely to provide harmony for such a couple is for them to do some things together and allow their partner to do other things alone.

Avoiding under-arousal may be accomplished like this.

TO INCREASE UNDER-AROUSAL

1 Participate in a number of varied activities and, by so doing, stay alert.

2 Take risks and thus challenge your skills.
3 Avoid isolation by actively seeking social interaction.
4 Update your knowledge to overcome obsolescence.
5 Stretch yourself by setting goals with a 50 per cent chance of success.

Occupants of the Drone Zone, should they wish to enhance their performance, need to seek challenge at the expense of mastery. That is why goals set at the 50 per cent level seem to motivate best. Should they be set too high, people tend to give up quickly; should they be set too low, boredom is the result.

Successful people seem able to achieve a reasonable balance between challenge and mastery, although they may not think of it in these terms. Most of us probably don't think about the idea at all, so perhaps the following exercise is worth doing.

CHALLENGE

- Think about previous times in your life when you took risks, challenging yourself to go beyond your normal bounds. Remember the excitement and anticipation of trying something new, the uncertainty of involving yourself in something a little out of your control. Recall the heightened arousal, the energy, the fear, the vitality which sharpened the intensity of your life.
- List some of the risks you have taken. As you do so, attempt to mentally recreate and re-experience the challenge in as much detail as you can.
- List the challenges you would like to take in the future, the risks you would like to accept.

MASTERY

- Think about previous times in your life when you achieved mastery. Remember the satisfaction you derived from doing something really well. Recall the sense of ease and confidence with which you did these things.

- List some of the areas in your life in which you have achieved mastery. As you do so, attempt to mentally recreate and re-experience the sense of competence in as much detail as you can.
- List areas in your life where you would like to develop more competence and expertise.

Something else you may like to do is to estimate whether your present job provides a reasonable balance between challenge and mastery. After you answer the questions in the scale on page 106, use the column headed 'SUM', to deduct your **b** response from your **a** response. This could be plus, zero, or minus. When you add these scores, if the total is between +3 and −3, you have a reasonable balance. A larger plus figure indicates your job could be pushing you into the Panic Zone while a larger minus figure suggests boredom with what you do is putting you into the Drone Zone.

COPING WITH DISTRESS

In this chapter I have taken a somewhat different tack from that presented in my book, *The Stress Factor*. That is because, for business people, emphasis falls primarily on optimizing performance in order to achieve success. I believe the C Zone concept is valuable in this context. However, it is important to take a close look at your definition of success once again. Where is it getting you? If it is, for example, inconsistent with good health, job satisfaction, and achievement of personal goals, perhaps it needs revision.

In a headlong rush for business success, for higher salaries, more responsibilities, a heavier work load, you may be subjecting yourself to an overload of stress. Though it may be perceived in other ways, stress is often defined as

YOUR JOB AND THE C ZONE

For each statement, circle the number expressing your honest opinion.

Statements	Little	Some	Average	More than average	A lot	SUM (a–b)
1 Number of deadlines						
(a) I have to meet.	1	2	3	4	5	
(b) I am capable of meeting.	1	2	3	4	5	_____
2 The extent to which my						
(a) abilities are used.	1	2	3	4	5	
(b) abilities could be used.	1	2	3	4	5	_____
3 The number of things						
(a) I have to do.	1	2	3	4	5	
(b) I am capable of doing.	1	2	3	4	5	_____
4 The level of difficulty						
(a) of my work.	1	2	3	4	5	
(b) I can handle.	1	2	3	4	5	_____
5 In a day, the amount of work						
(a) I have to do.	1	2	3	4	5	
(b) I am able to do.	1	2	3	4	5	_____
6 The quality of work						
(a) I have to do.	1	2	3	4	5	
(b) I am capable of doing.	1	2	3	4	5	_____
7 The number of people I						
(a) have to work with.	1	2	3	4	5	
(b) would like to work with.	1	2	3	4	5	_____
8 The level of complexity						
(a) of the tasks I do.	1	2	3	4	5	
(b) I am able to handle.	1	2	3	4	5	_____
9 The number of projects						
(a) I have to do.	1	2	3	4	5	
(b) I am capable of doing.	1	2	3	4	5	_____
10 The responsibility						
(a) of my present job.	1	2	3	4	5	
(b) I am able to handle.	1	2	3	4	5	_____

the body's response to any demands placed upon it. When these demands are interpreted as threatening, you will experience distress. Therefore, to relieve this distress it becomes necessary to reduce the threat you perceive in your environment.

Coping with distress, then, comes down to controlling your mental processes for, as I have pointed out earlier, it is not the events which happen that are distressing, but our reactions to those events. Let's look at some ways of achieving this control.

Doing things in the present instead of putting them off to the future is a basic principle both of successful living and reducing distress. Exist in the 'now'. Enjoy what is happening at this moment rather than allowing yourself to become preoccupied with the past or the future. At times we can enjoy the past and look forward to the future, but it is easy to allow such thinking to dominate. When it does, we fail to recognize and seize the many opportunities which exist in the 'here and now'.

The present is all we have. The past is gone. The future has not yet arrived. In fact, someone once commented that the nicest thing about the future is that it only comes one day at a time. When we wake in the morning we are given the gift of a new day, a fresh unspoilt life. It stretches ahead of us, allowing us, within quite considerable limits, to fashion it in the way we desire.

It takes self-discipline to live in this way. Constantly we have to drag our minds away from the backward looking phrase, 'If only I hadn't . . .', and the forward portent of disaster, 'What would happen if . . .'. Most of the things about which we worry never actually happen, so we remove a lot of distress and pressure by living one day at a time. Each night, leave behind today's problems and mentally visualize a successful new day tomorrow. In this way, you avoid the pitfall of starting each day by taking up yesterday's burden and anticipating today's troubles. That is a certain recipe for spoiling the new day before you even get started.

Together with living one day at a time, the other key principle is to **put your own meaning on events**, to label things in a way that is beneficial to you. If we label something as a pressure-inducing threat, then we will experience distress. However, if we choose to use a different label, we are able to transform that feeling. Ken Bailey did this is a very dramatic way.

Ken, the 43-year-old manager of a wholesale liquor business, began having panic attacks. These were so severe that, should one occur while he was driving, he would have to pull over to the side of the road and stay there until it passed. On occasions, this could take up to half an hour. Sometimes he would experience panic while he was at work, this rendering him temporarily incapable of doing anything at all.

These attacks were actually triggered by Ken's thinking. He had developed a sense of discomfort in his chest and, despite reassurances from both general practictioners and specialists, the meaning he assigned to this symptom was: 'I've got something wrong with my heart. I'm going to have a heart attack and die.' When he thought like this, he usually triggered off a panic attack.

Ken had recently begun windsurfing, and he told me that this sport had become his greatest joy in life. I was able to use this piece of information to help Ken change the meaning he was attaching to his physical symptom. Whenever he felt the chest discomfort, I encouraged Ken to immediately imagine himself windsurfing.

Often we are able to derive almost as much pleasure from imagining ourselves doing something that we enjoy doing as if we were actually doing it. This was certainly true of Ken, who was now using his chest pain as a trigger to think of something enjoyable rather than to think of something frightening. Once he made this change, his panic attacks ceased. Though he still possesses the physical symptom, he has changed the way he labels it and, by so doing, has removed an area of distress from his life.

We all have this power. There is no real world 'out

there'. The real world exists in our own minds. This mean we have the power to change our worlds by changing the way we think, by assigning different, more positive meanings to events which have previously caused distress. This is the key to coping successfully with stress, though there are many other ways, too, of controlling our mental processes.

Laughing at yourself helps a lot. Most of us take ourselves far too seriously. We have a penchant for making mountains out of molehills, and then worrying about the great problems we have thus created. Catch yourself out doing this, then laugh at yourself for acting in such a way. If you can't do this yourself, encourage your spouse, children, and friends to do so. If you initially resent being 'rubbished', console yourself with the thought that we only 'rubbish' people we like.

Compartmentalizing is useful, too. This was another technique I encouraged Ken to use. All that it involves is putting away in a mental compartment those things which cannot be dealt with at the moment. Ken used an elaborate fantasy of a large castle with many rooms. Different things were put away in different rooms. He found it quite a useful way of easing distress.

Developing a positive addiction, mentioned earlier as one of the characteristics of the effective individual, helps too. The idea here is to reduce stress by becoming immersed in an activity such as jogging or meditation. It seems to work best if the activity, whatever it may be, takes no longer than one hour a day, can be done easily without much mental effort, and can be done alone. You will tend to become more involved if you believe you will improve in some way or another if you keep at it.

However, don't fall prey to self-criticism, being hard on yourself if you are unable to achieve the improvement you expect. That will defeat the whole purpose of the exercise. Become absorbed if you can, but be kind to yourself as you do. Unfortunately, this is something that many Type A individuals are unable to do, yet they are the very people who are most at risk from the deleterious effects of stress.

THE TYPE A INDIVIDUAL

If only one word could be used to define the Type A personality, that word would probably be 'aggressive'. It sums up the willingness to take risks, to engage in direct action, to be bold, energetic, pushing, to seize the initiative and to be enterprising. In the main, these all seem to be highly desirable qualities for one who wishes to succeed in business. Unfortunately, they are also the qualities which make such a person a prime candidate for heart attacks.

Fortunately, there are ways in which Type A individuals, while still maintaining their energetic drive and ability to get things done, can break the bad habits which cause them to be a health risk. One of these ways is to make a deliberate, conscious effort to **hear what other people are saying**. This will reduce the tendency to speak and think too rapidly. Every time a Type A individual feels the urge to finish someone else's sentence, he or she could, with profit, take a slow, deep breath instead.

Most of us find it difficult to listen because we believe that what we have to say is more important than what other people have to say. Sometimes we may be right, but not as often as we think we are. As Epictetus has pointed out, we have been given two ears but only one mouth so that we may listen at least twice as much as we speak.

Observe the people who are really influential at meetings and conferences. Most of them weigh their words with care. They will usually wait, listening to what others have to say, perhaps asking the occasional question, then quietly, simply, and forcefully they will put their own viewpoint. This approach works much better than that of the constant talker who, even when he or she does come up with a good idea, is ignored because the quality material is lost in the morass of verbal garbage. Too many of us suffer from 'verbal diarrhoea', a very counterproductive complaint. By slowing down and listening a little more, we not only begin to counter the Type A habit of doing things too fast but we are also likely to increase our own effectiveness.

As part of the 'doing things too fast' habit, Type A individuals attempt to do several things at once. To counteract this habit, it is necessary to really concentrate on **doing only one thing at a time**. If you normally work on other tasks while waiting for a phone call to be answered, deliberately choose to relax, to close your eyes and take a few deep breaths, or to gaze out of the window. This may seem difficult at first. You may even feel guilty about it, thinking of what you could be doing. However, if you are realistic, you will realize that you actually accomplish very little by trying to do several things at once. It is likely that the short relaxation break may refresh you so you work better after your phone call.

It is all a matter of time pressure really. Type A individuals make into a fetish the belief that every second is precious, that it is a sin to be doing nothing. Often this thinking is counterproductive because the stress engendered pushes them into the Panic Zone where not only does performance deteriorate dramatically but the risk of serious illness increases markedly.

To reduce some of this, usually self-imposed, time pressure, **allow yourself more time than you think you need** to get a job completed. You will not only feel less stressed but will, in all probability, produce better work. Perhaps, if you are able to begin your day fifteen minutes earlier than normal, you can use this time for something you enjoy. This could be as simple as a walk before breakfast, leisurely reading the newspaper, or chatting with your family.

It is helpful to make your lunch 'hour' a break from work, too. Research on the factory floor demonstrates clearly that workers produce more when they are given **frequent breaks**. If you insist on working through lunch time, constantly rushing, your performance will deteriorate. A break at lunch time can provide the respite necessary for you to recharge your batteries.

Many years ago I found that I was unable to do anything creative during the early afternoon hours. I handled mechanical tasks satisfactorily but anything more demanding seemed to be beyond me. Yet, once I started taking a respite during the middle of the day, this problem disappeared. The way I used this break was that, in addition to eating lunch, I took the previously desribed 10 minute 'mental holiday', and a short walk, all in the space of an hour.

Another way of using the lunch break, or any other respite you feel necessary to give yourself, is to practice the **'relaxation response'** described by Benson and Klipper in their book of the same name. They claim that there is nothing new about this technique, rather that it is a 'scientific validation of age old wisdom'. Whether that is true or not, many people have found a greatly increased sense of calm and relaxation through using the method on a regular basis. Because they work easier, without great stress or anxiety, their performance tends to improve.

THE RELAXATION RESPONSE TECHNIQUE

1 Sit quietly in a comfortable position.
2 Close your eyes.
3 Deeply relax all muscles, beginning at your feet and progressing up to your face. Keep them relaxed.
4 Breathe through your nose. Become aware of your breathing. As you breathe out, say the word 'ONE' silently to yourself. For example, breathe in . . . out, 'ONE'; in . . . out, 'ONE'. Breathe easily, naturally.
5 Continue for ten or twenty minutes. You may open your eyes to check the time, but do not use an alarm. When you finish, sit quietly for several minutes, at first with your eyes closed and later with your eyes opened. Do not stand up for a few minutes.

6 Do not worry whether you are successful in achieving a deep level of relaxation. Maintain a passive attitude and permit relaxation to occur at its own pace. When distracting thoughts occur, try to ignore them by not dwelling upon them and return to repeating 'ONE'. With practice, the response should come with little effort. Practice the techniques once or twice daily, but not within two hours after any meal, since the digestive processes seem to inferfere with the relaxation response.

STRESS ANALYSIS

Just as a Time Log is useful to clarify how you use your time, so a **Stress Log** is a valuable indicator of the stress that is in your life. Sometimes this comes from a single dramatic incident. On other occasions it stems from a cumulation of minor, less emotion-fraught, related incidents. Whatever its source, you can become aware of its presence by keeping, for one week, the following record.

STRESS LOG

At the end of each day describe:
- the most stressful single incident that occurred;
- the most stressful series of related incidents that occurred;
- the approximate stress level of your day on a rating scale of 'one' (not very stressful) to 'ten' (extremely stressful).

Another way of sharpening your awareness of the stress in your life is to do the following simple analysis.

1 List the things that produce distress in your life.
2 For each item note:
- WHO is involved in your distress?
- WHERE does this distress occur?

- HOW FREQUENTLY does this distress occur?
- Do you feel as if you have any CONTROL in the situation?

3 Put a √ next to those distressful situations to which there seems to be a remedy.

4 Put a * next to the three items you would most like to resolve.

Armed with the information furnished by your Stress Log and Stress Analysis, you can take action to reduce the distress level of your life. This is really a matter of handling pressure more successfully than you are already doing.

An effective way of doing this is to recognize what is within your control and what is not. Concentrate your energies upon what you can do instead of wasting effort by worrying about what you can't do. When under pressure, stop, take a few deep breaths while counting to ten, then check the situation creating the problem.

1 Identify those factors over which you have some control. For these, consider what you CAN DO to improve matters.

2 For those factors over which you do not have control, consider what you CAN DO to improve upon the situation.

3 Arrange these CAN DOs in order of priority and you have a plan of action which is likely to be very effective in reducing the pressure on you.

This method and others outlined in this chapter will have given you some ideas on how you might manage stress more successfully. However, this is only one aspect of staying healthy. The next chapter looks at other approaches to health and healing.

8 Your Good Health

THE IMPORTANCE OF RELAXATION

In the previous chapter, great store was placed on relaxation as a way of coping with stress more successfully. Its importance goes beyond this, for the ability to relax would seem to be an essential ingredient of good health generally. Many of us realize that we have great difficulty in letting go. Others do not even realize that they go through life tense and anxious, wondering why they feel so tired, why their limbs ache so frequently, why everything is such an effort. By remaining unaware of their tension, such people accept their state as the norm, and thus their life is far less enjoyable than it otherwise could be.

Answering the following questions will give you a rough guide to your ability to relax.

YOUR ABILITY TO RELAX

Circle the number below indicating how often you experience each of the following situations (3 = often; 2 = sometimes; 1 = rarely)

	Often	Sometimes	Rarely
1 Are you able to concentrate on what you are doing without worrying about other things?	3	2	1

---

2 Is it possible for you to relax once you have found the time to do so?	3	2	1
3 Are you able to forget about your worries when you go to bed at night?	3	2	1
4 Are you able to take a nap during the day and wake up refreshed?	3	2	1
5 Do you find time to relax and stretch during the day?	3	2	1
6 Do you make frequent checks on whether you are scowling, clenching your fists, furrowing your brow, hunching your shoulders, or tightening you jaw?	3	2	1
7 Are you able to relax so that you can sleep easily and deeply?	3	2	1
8 Do you know how to release tension when you feel under too much pressure?	3	2	1
9 When you play, do you become completely absorbed in what you are doing?	3	2	1
10 Do you plan your life to include change of people, scenery, activities, thoughts?	3	2	1
Total	_____	_____	_____

Score of 23–30 = high ability to relax
17–22 = average ability to relax
10–16 = low ability to relax

From your score on this scale, you will derive some idea of whether you need to put into practice the various relaxation techniques described in this book. However, even if you already cope with your life in a reasonably relaxed manner, there are other things you may like to consider as possible ways of improving your health. One of these is the control of pain.

PAIN CONTROL

Although there is a physical element involved in pain, we have the power to increase or decrease its effect. Pain is essentially your reaction to sensations which you perceived as hurting, and it is possible to modify these reactions. When a young boy, for example, has a fall from his tricycle, he is likely to scream and cry. His mother rushes to comfort him, cuddling him in her arms, perhaps feeding him a sweet. The cries soon diminish, and off he goes again, happily riding his tricycle once more. In fact, if, after his fall, the boy realizes his mother is not within earshot, he is unlikely to cry at all. He brushes off his 'injury' and continues playing.

Adults are the same. Our minds often act as amplifiers, increasing the severity of pain by focusing our attention upon it. On other occasions, they act as dampers, suppressing our consciousness of pain to the extent that we are virtually unaware of discomfort.

When I have worked as a sports psychologist for football teams, I have often been amazed at the way in which seriously injured players continue playing, not becoming aware of their injuries until after the game. If our minds have the power to naturally suppress consciousness of pain during times of conflict and competition, it would be very helpful for us to invoke this mechanism voluntarily to minimize pain whenever we wanted to. This is not only possible, it is far easier than most people imagine.

Some time ago I had as a patient a nine-year-old boy, Tom, who was suffering from leukemia. The form of treatment he was having, bone marrow aspirations, upset him greatly. The week before his aspiration, he would frequently wake during the night with frightful nightmares. Through fear, he would vomit and have diarrhoea. While actually having the aspiration he would scream and cry, struggling against the nurses who would have to hold him down.

I had only one session with Tom. He was an amazing little boy who understood immediately how he could change the way he felt about his treatment. Though I showed him a number of different ways he could distract his mind from what was being done to his body, the one he found most interesting was the Zen breathing technique described earlier. This involved imagining numbers on the in breath and taking these down to the body centre on the out breath.

Tom adapted this technique to suit his own interests. As he breathed in, he imagined an aeroplane flying in one side of his mind and parachuting out a number as it reached the centre. As he breathed out, he imagined the parachute, with the number hanging under it, drifting down until it came to rest just below his navel. He would do ten of these, then start again.

A few weeks later his mother rang me. Apparently, from the time he left me, Tom assured her that he would have no further trouble with the aspirations. He 'knew' how to handle them. Indeed he did. For the week preceeding the treatment, he was quite calm, no nightmares, no vomiting, no diarrhoea. At the hospital, he solemnly told the doctor he would be 'going away' for a while and would the doctor tap him on the arm when he was finished so he would know when to come back again. He then closed his eyes, to better concentrate on his plane and parachutes.

The doctor and nurses found it hard to believe their ears. They found it even harder to believe their eyes when Tom, this screaming, shouting child of previous treatment sessions, remained calm during the whole procedure, showing no sign of pain whatever. When he had completed the treatment, the doctor tapped Tom on the arm. He opened his eyes, thanked the doctor, and walked out quietly with his mother.

This might sound like a fairy tale, but it is true. Tom had learned, and learned very quickly, to hypnotize himself, to achieve a separation of mind and body. He is not unique in being able to do this. Many terminally ill cancer patients are able to do without pain killing medication by using similar **dissociation** techniques to distance themselves from their pain. Thus they are able to spend the little time they have left interacting with their families, their senses not dulled by pain killers.

Not everyone is, of course, able to dissociate their minds and bodies as successfully as these people. Because the needs of the terminally ill are so great, and their emotions so strong, they usually achieve deep levels of self-hypnosis very quickly. Really severe pain is a great spur to rapid learning.

I've found this also applies to pregnant women who have had a previously painful childbirth. Many of them are able to dissociate very successfully so that, during childbirth, they imagine themselves leaving the body of the woman on the delivery table, sitting down on a chair across the room, and not getting back into their body until the baby has been born. They feel no pain. That is all experienced by the woman on the delivery table from whom they have temporarily separated.

Such dissociation is one way in which our minds enable us to suppress pain. A less complete detachment of mind from body is seen with **distraction**. This involves thinking about something other that what is happening now, putting yourself in a different situation.

A hospital administrator, Terry Wheeler, who attended

a health and healing workshop I conducted recently found that imaginatively immersing himself in his favourite sport, skiing, was an answer to the anxiety he used to feel in the dentist's chair. As the dentist prodded and probed, drilled and polished, Terry sped down the slopes, travelled on ski lifts, performed intricate turns and manoeuvres, and even enjoyed an après-ski schnapps. Absorbed in his imaginings, Terry was able to occupy his mind so that he no longer concentrated on the discomforts of the dental procedures. As it was this concentration which had previously amplified pain sensations, he was now able to undergo dental treatment with far more equanimity.

Going away to a special place is also a method of absorbing the mind so it will not notice pain. This is another use for the 'mental holiday' idea. Mentally, you remove yourself from a situation where your are experiencing pain to another situation which has pleasant connotations. If you can combine both imagery and sound, the method is likely to be even more effective.

A dentist of my acquaintance teaches his younger patients to do this. First, he has them think of a particular place they would like to be. When they can imagine this, he has them raise the index finger of their right hand. Then he has them hear a piece of music they like, beating time with the index finger of their left hand. He proceeds with dental work, keeping an eye on the two fingers as he does so. As long as one is raised and the other beating time, he is confident his patients are feeling no pain. However, should either finger drop, he stops immediately and encourages the patient to re-establish the image and the sound.

Such **goal-directed imaginings** create fantasies that are incompatible with pain. A particularly useful one is to imagine Novocaine being painlessly injected into an injured part of the body to dull the discomfort. Another is the phantom limb fantasy. If you have a very painful leg, you would imagine a phantom leg containing all the pain slowly rising from your body, separating, drifting away further and further, until it finally disappeared, taking with it all discomfort.

Many other fantasies for overcoming pain appear in another book of mine, *The Fantasy Factor*. I draw attention to the approach again here as it can be extremely effective. Unfortunately, it is one that is overlooked by most people, just as they overlook the power of **direct suggestion** in banishing pain. By telling ourselves that we hurt, and concentrating on that sensation, we create increased pain. This could be termed negative self-hypnosis. Many of us are very good at it. It follows that we would be just as good at positive self-hypnosis if only we would give ourselves a chance to practise it.

Terry Wheeler, the imaginative skiier of the previous example, was initially an unbeliever who now practises enthusiastically. On a recent skiing trip, he fell awkwardly, injuring his ankle. While waiting for help, he repeated over and over a litany that went something like this: 'My ankle is feeling more and more comfortable. There is an increasing sense of ease. It is cool and easy.' He avoided mentioning pain, using the word 'comfort' instead. That is a good policy, to use the positive word and not the negative one.

Use of positive direct suggestion promotes a sense of increased **relaxation**. Pain never seems as bad when we are relaxed, in marked contrast to the increase in discomfort we feel when we are anxious and tense. It has been suggested, in this context, that the most useful thing heart attack victims can do is to stay as quiet as possible, calming themselves with direct suggestions of increasing ease, comfort, and relaxation. Behaving in this way modifies the usual panic reaction which aggravates the physical symptom.

One interesting technique reportedly used by some ambulance officers is teaching patients to reduce pain through use of a **pain scale**. They have their patients tell them, on a scale of zero (no pain) to ten (unbearable pain), where they are at the moment. Patients are asked to imagine this number up in the corner of their minds. Once they can do so, they are to gradually change it. If the starting number was eight, they would slowly change the curves of the eight into straight lines so it took on the shape of a seven. These lines would, in turn, give way to the curves of a six, and so on until the pain was brought to a more bearable level. This technique involves aspects of distraction, relaxation, and direct suggestion. So too does this little exercise.

PAIN RELIEF

- Lie down, close your eyes, and relax deeply. Focus on your breath, breathing deeply, slowly and naturally. Count down slowly from ten to one, feeling yourself drifting into a deeper, more relaxed state with each count.
- When deeply relaxed, imagine a brightly coloured sphere of light about 15 cm in diameter. 'See' it gradually growing bigger and bigger until it fills your mind.
- Now 'see' it shrinking, becoming smaller and smaller until it returns to its original size. Let it become smaller still, shrinking more and more until it finally disappears completely.
- Repeat this process of visualization, this time imagining the brightly coloured sphere is your pain.

By giving pain a size, you make it concrete. Once you have done so, you can manipulate it. No longer is it vague and amorphous. This is also true when you use colour rather than size.

HEALING TECHNIQUES

When I was in New York recently, I was making the rounds of publishing houses. As I like to walk, I didn't take cabs so, by the end of the day, I had walked many miles on hard pavements. When I awoke the next morning, my feet were so painful that walking was difficult. As I had many more calls to make, this situation was not one I desired.

To improve matters I used the healing power of the **colour change**. I located the three areas on my feet which were causing the most distress and, as I concentrated on them, the colour red seemed to be present. I then focused on a part of my body, my shoulder, which felt comfortable and strong. The colour blue was present here. I switched my concentration back to the painful areas, changing the red into blue. This took a few minutes but, when I had accomplished this, the feet felt far more comfortable. Throughout the next half-hour, as I walked the streets of New York, I had to keep making this colour switch each time any pain returned, but, by the end of that time, the healing was complete and I had no further trouble.

Sometimes, when I describe this healing technique to people, they will claim they are unable to imagine any colour associated with their injury. On these occasions I ask: 'If a colour was there, what would it be?' Almost immediately I get a reply. The colour is there but, initially, we may not be aware of its presence.

Changing colour is often a very effective approach to healing. So is **image changing**. Janine Walters, a graphic artist in an advertising agency, regularly gets 'knots' in her shoulders after long sessions at the drawing board. Stretching and exercising provide some relief but she achieves her best results from mentally 'untying the knots'.

This healing technique can be used whenever you are able to imagine your injury or physical symptom in some way that is capable of change. This may be visual, such as a tightly knotted rope or a dirty pool of stagnant water. It could be auditory if a sound, such as grinding or gurgling, is associated with the problem. Maybe a texture is involved, with a sore throat feeling like rough sandpaper, or perhaps temperature is present in a hot headache or an icy feeling in the pit of the stomach. Sometimes smells or tastes can be invoked. On other occasions movement, such as pounding or stabbing, might be part of the imaginative creation.

Once you have described the symptom in one or more of the ways mentioned above, use your imagination to decide what it will be like when it is alleviated or cured. This usually involves substituting for the original image one that is its opposite. The knotted ropes are untied; the stagnant pool is drained and replaced by clear, sweet water; the gurgling subsides to a gentle murmur; the throat is smoothed out with a coating of glycerine; ice packs cool the headache; and the pounding movement is replaced by the gentle lapping of waves on the shore.

You may find that using words to accompany the image make it stronger: 'My throat is becoming quite comfortable as the glycerine spreads with silky smoothness', or 'My head is light and free, full of billowy, white clouds.' Do whatever seems appropriate for you to make your images vibrant and effective. Then you can use them immediately a physical symptom surfaces.

You may care to **create an inner guide** to offer advice on how to treat such physical symptoms. Go on a mental journey, firstly into a beautiful meadow, then climbing a mountain which rises out of this meadow, and finally into some form of temple located at the top of the mountain. Inside the temple, you meet your advisor. Alternatively, your journey may take you down into the earth. As you enter a cave, you may find your advisor sitting beside a fire waiting for you.

Use your imagination to experiment, creating different situations. Either allow your mind to provide an advisor for you, or deliberately try out different ones—humans, animals, spirits—until you find one with whom you are comfortable. Then ask questions about your health, and wait quietly for answers. You usually get them, and, on many occasions, the advice is remarkably perceptive.

What you are doing is, metaphorically, getting in touch with your own unconscious, a part of your mind which is supposed to retain in its memory everything that happens to you. Thus, it has vastly more knowledge on which to draw than is provided by the more limited memory of the conscious mind.

Instead of, or in addition to, conversing with your advisor, you may also wish to talk to a part of your body which is causing you problems. The following exercise, based on one suggested by Jean Houston in *The Possible Human*, could help you do so.

GETTING PREPARED

- Using pen and paper, or talking either to yourself or out loud, recall the problem.
- With closed eyes, breathe deeply, and rest for a few minutes.
- Open your eyes.

SETTING THE STAGE

- Either talking to yourself or out loud, or perhaps using pen and paper, go back over the history of the problem as if it were the personal 'life story' or a person you have known:
  - When was the problem born?
  - How and where did it grow?
  - What have been the high and low points in its life?
  - When does it come to visit you?
- Rest with eyes closed for a few minutes.

THE CONVERSATION

- Imagine the problem sitting in a chair across the room from you.
- Give it a name.
- As quickly as you can, without stopping to reread or edit, write out a conversation between yourself and the probelm.

If you are interested in modifying your dreams, you could use a variant of this idea. Have paper and pen available beside your bed. When you wake, either during the night or in the morning with a dream still fresh in your mind, write it down in as much detail as you can remember. Then, in turn, become each of the people, animals, and objects in the dream, speaking as if you were they. Develop conversations between them. If you do so, the meaning of your dream will become readily apparent. This can be quite useful, for dreams frequently provide valuable information on important aspects of our lives, including our health.

THE VALUE OF CENTERING

You have probably observed that most of the exercises which involve use of the imagination or which facilitate relaxation begin with a period of quiet, slow breathing. One of the main reasons for this is to help you become centred, a process which involves shifting awareness away from your ever-active mind, with its constant babble of conflicting thoughts, to a part of your body where where more stillness prevails.

This body centre is often regarded as being located about four centimetres below the navel. That is why the technique of pain control I taught Tom, the boy with leukemia, involved him in a shift of focus from his mind to this navel area. However, people differ in the exact location of their centres. If you want to find your own centre, these suggestions will help.

- Take a few slow, very deep breaths. From where does the breath come? To what point does the deepest breath reach?
- Imagine that your body is a house. In one room of this house you feel most at home, comfortable and relax. Where would this room be?
- If you think of yourself as having a soul, a spirit, an inner essence, where in your body would it be?

- Pretend that you are attempting to balance your body around a central point. Where would it be?
- Say 'I am me' several times while pointing to yourself. To what part of your body are you pointing? What place in your body feels truest?

Finding your centre can be very useful. By concentrating upon this area, and breathing into it, you establish, quite rapidly, a sense of calm. This is particularly valuable when you are feeling harassed and need to steady yourself. It is also of use on occasions when you are ill or injured, and your anxiety is interfering with the body's normal healing process. When you breathe slowly and deeply, sending those breaths to your centre, you create an environment more conducive to successful healing.

In fact, the concept of breathing into your centre can be extended more widely. Should some part of your body be injured, deliberately direct your breath to that area. As you breathe out, imagine the breath flowing into the injury, warm and soothing, bring comfort and relief. Linking this idea with the colour healing suggested earlier can by a very powerful means of speeding recovery.

Many of the athletes with whom I work have adopted this method with great success. Initially, they had to overcome considerable scepticism, for the concept is not one with which they were at all familiar. Yet those who were prepared to give it a try reaped considerable benefits. Injuries healed faster, felt more comfortable, interfered less with their lives. Also, quite apart form treating a particular problem, a number of them use it in the following way to create a sense of wellbeing.

BODY REGENERATION

- Sit comfortably, arms and legs uncrossed, letting go so that the chair supports your weight. With eyes closed, concentrate on the end of your nose, imagining what your breath looks like as you draw it in, then mentally follow it down into your lungs. 'See' it swirling about in your lungs, then, as you breathe out, feel the air leaving your body, carrying with it tension, pain, and illness. Continue for a couple of minutes.

- Concentrate on the centre of your abdomen, imagining a tiny opening there through which you are breathing. 'See' the oxygen flowing in, swirling around in your abdomen, lower back, anal, and genital areas, then flowing out as you let go the breath. Again, imagine it carrying away tension and discomfort as you do this for a minute or two.

- Shift your focus to the centre of your chest in the heart region. 'See' a tiny door opening there so that, as you inhale, you draw oxygen into your chest, heart and upper body generally. It circulates through this area, then, as you exhale, carries away discomfort and strain.

- Breathe in and out through the centre of your forehead, each exhalation bringing the sense of comfort in your face and brain.

- Continue this process, moving through the body, base of the spine, genitals, palms of the hands, and anywhere else that seems appropriate. Concentrate particularly on any area that is suffering disease or pain.

- Conclude by breathing naturally with every cell of your body until you are ready to stretch and open your eyes.

HOMOEOPATHY

In my work as a psychotherapist, I have found homoeopathic remedies a useful adjunct to other forms of treatment. These remedies appear to help people improve their health without the fear of unwanted side effects. In *The Healing Factor* I have discussed the theory of this form of self-help medicine in some detail. Here we can briefly consider the value of homoeopathic remedies in the treatment of depression, anxiety, phobias, and grief. When we suffer from such mental complaints, our performance is adversely affected, preventing us from achieving the success we seek.

Many businessmen and women, for example, suffer from 'nerves' when they are in any test-like situation such as giving presentations to their peers, negotiating with employees, and explaining to superiors why particular decisions have been made. Taking **Argentum nitricum** the evening before the test-like situation, and again the next morning, is often sufficient to remove the 'nerves' symptom. It seems to work particularly well, too, for agoraphobics and those who are afraid of heights, though, in these cases, it is preferable to take the remedy three times a day between meals over a period of time.

'Nerves' are primarily generated through fear of the impending event, a fear which generates agitation, sweating, accelerated heartbeat, and dry throat. Where Argentum nitricum fails to achieve the desired anxiety reduction, another well-tried homoeopathic remedy, **Gelsemium**, will probably effect a 'cure'.

Though both these remedies may prove useful in case of depression, my first choice for a patient in this state would be **Aurum metallicum**. It has been called the 'remedy of deepest despair', possibly because it can be so effective in cases where people are suicidal.

Should the problem be more a matter of mood swings, which cause difficulties for both the individuals involved and the associates with whom they work, **Pulsatilla** is likely to be helpful in reducing these to more manageable proportions. Should this remedy prove ineffective, then **Ignatia** may prove more successful. It works well when a person alternates rapidly between cheerfulness and depression, and is a marvellous remedy when grief is an important component of the problem.

Though grieving over loss is necessary, sometimes this may continue for so long that it interferes with a person's life. Should this be the case, use of Ignatia may help to restore the balance which has been temporarily lost.

This is true of many mental difficulties. Chris Jacobs, the manager of a picture theatre, is, on most occasions an affable man, competent at his job. Except when he loses his temper. His violence then is out of all proportion to whatever has triggered the outburst. His temper looked like it would cost him his job. Fortunately, he found that **Nux Vomica**, provided an answer. If it had not achieved the moderation of temper he wanted, Chris could have tried **Hepar Sulph**. Both these remedies offer help for oversensitive people who give vent to destructive feelings in a way that is causing harm to themselves and to others around them.

Less violent than Ken, Andrew, his brother, has a different problem which is disrupting his previously successful career as a stockbroker. He has become irritable, discontented, and quarrelsome. This attitude loses him clients. People simply do not want to listen to complaints. Unlike Ken, Andrew is unwilling to explore the possible benefits of homoeopathy. If he did, it is possible that **Silica**, **Psorinum** or **Chamomilla** would help him moderate his irritability. This latter remedy is often used in extreme cases, for it helps the individual to whom everything is intolerable.

By talking of using particular remedies to alleviate specific problems, I am contradicting conventional homoeopathic practice in which a detailed history helps the practitioner to identify the patient's individual constitiutional remedy. In this way, it is the patient who is treated, not the symptom. However, although I do prefer to work in this manner by attempting to locate the remedy most suitable to the individual, I have also found that some remedies have emerged as specifics for the relief of particular symptoms. The ones mentioned above do seem to help most people who have the mental symtoms I have described.

THE BACH FLOWER REMEDIES

Similarily, the Bach flower remedies may be used quite safely to alleviate a wide variety of problems which interfere with the successful pursuance of a career. Based on the premise that it is our anxieties and fear which open up our bodies to the invasion of disease, Edward Bach developed a system of 'medicine' capable of promoting healing without the creation of adverse side-effects. He theorized that the basis of disease lay in the disharmony of conflicting moods which produced unhappiness, mental torture, fear, self-doubt, and resignation. Such disharmony lowered the body's vitality, permitting illness to flourish. Accordingly, Bach chose to develop remedies which would modify mood and temperament rather than those directed towards the amelioration of physical symptoms. Some of the more useful of these are:

- **Aspen** for vague fears of unknown origin, anxiety, apprehension.
- **Beech** for intolerance, an over-critical attitude, irritability.
- **Cerato** for self-distrust and doubt of one's own ability.
- **Crab Apple** for the cleansing of mind and body, self-disgust.
- **Gentian** for those who are easily discouraged, doubt, depression.
- **Holly** for hatred, envy, jealousy, suspicion, resentment.
- **Hornbeam** for mental and physical exhaustion.
- **Impatiens** for impatience, irritability, extreme mental tension.
- **Larch** for lack of confidence, anticipation of failure, despondency.
- **Mimulus** for fear or anxiety of a known origin.
- **Mustard** for black depression, melancholia, gloom.

- **Pine** for overconscientiousness, self-reproach, guilt feelings.
- **Scleranthus** for uncertainty, indecision, changeability of moods.
- **White Chestnut** for persistent unwanted thoughts, worries.
- **The Rescue Remedy**, a mixture of five remedies which is valuable in an emergency to treat shock, fright, or severe pain.

Both homoeopathic and Bach remedies will either help you or do nothing at all. They will not harm you. However, the same cannot be said for food.

YOU ARE WHAT YOU EAT

It does seem reasonable to eat in a way which promotes good rather than bad health. The difficulty is to know how to do this. We are confronted by so much conflicting evidence that it is difficult to come to any definite conclusions. That which one authority prescribes, another equally well qualified refutes.

A synthesis of present thinking on diet would suggest that it is wise to reduce our intake of some foods and increase our intake of others. The **Healthy Diet Pyramid** summarizes this information.

THE HEALTHY DIET PYRAMID

EAT LEAST	Sugar	Butter	Margarine	Oil

EAT MODERATELY	Milk	Cheese	Yoghurt

Lean meat   Poultry   Fish   Legumes   Nuts
Eggs

EAT
MOST   Cereals   Bread   Vegetables   Fruit

Knowing what to eat to achieve and maintain good health can be something of a problem. In fact, life is full of problems which, if welcomed as challenges, can enliven our lives. This is particularly so if we have in our repertoire some techniques which enable us to solve them successfully.

9 Decision Making and Problem Solving

INFORMATION-GAINING TOOLS

To solve problems and make successful decisions it is necessary to have access to appropriate information. This sounds simple. Often it is not. Sometimes we find it difficult to pin down what information we actually do need to make our decision. On other occasions, we may know what we need but do not ask the correct questions to bring forth the information. There are times, too, when our questions do get at what we want but we misunderstand the material provided. This is usually because we assume that other people use language as we do, and we do not check to ascertain whether this is true or not. This assumption that we all define the same words in the same way can be disastrous to clear understanding.

Fortunately, there are tools which enable us to gain high quality information upon which to base our decisions and problem solutions. In their book, *Precision*, McMaster and Grinder use the labels 'frames, procedures, and pointers' to describe them. To see how these tools work in practice, consider a situation in which a firm making machine parts is now losing money. Six months ago, this firm was operating profitably. The firm's top executives are meeting to discover the reason for the existing loss, and to decide on remedial action.

FRAMES

Frames, three in number, are the first tool, their use being to clarify the limits of the discussion. The **outcome frame** is concerned with establishing a target and with providing criteria by which to evaluate what is relevant. In other words, this frame is used to decide on the precise objective of the meeting and can be expressed as:

(i) deciding why we are now losing money, and
(ii) deciding what action or actions to take to restore profitability.

Once these targets are set, all information brought forth must contribute to their achievement or else it is rejected.

As discussion proceeds, it is necessary to continually evaluate progress towards the target. This is the **backtrack frame**, a process of recapitulating information to ensure that it is relevant to the outcome established by the previous frame. Without such review, it is possible to drift off the track without realizing it.

Though the goal is clear and the information raised relevant to the achievement of that goal, stumbling blocks constantly arise. The **as-if frame** is designed to handle these. It is a tool for enabling the executives to act as if there are no limits on their proposals, as if the particular stumbling block has already been overcome. Perhaps the difficulty involves a man not present in the meeting. One of the executives who knows this man well might be invited to fill his shoes, to act as if he was that person, seeing the problem from his viewpoint. This prevents proceedings grinding to a halt.

Another way in which this frame may be used is for the participants in the discussion to act as if the outcome has already been achieved. That is, they assume the meeting has been successful in deciding why profits are down and what steps need to be taken to remedy the situation. The question is then asked: 'What needed to be done for us to have achieved this target decision?' In this way, effective procedures may be identified.

This is a technique I have found very useful in helping people solve all sorts of problems. I remember a woman, Jennie Fitzgerald, owner of an interior design business, who was very worried over a cash flow problem to which she could find no solution. I asked her to imagine herself going into the future, say two weeks hence, when the problem is solved. Then I asked Jennie to tell me what she had done to arrive at her solution, something she then proceeded to do without giving it a second thought. Suddenly she stopped, realizing what she was doing. The expression on her face was beautiful to see. She just couldn't believe it, but the solution was workable, one she could put into immediate action to solve her problem.

Jennie is not unusual in knowing more than she thought she knew. So often I find people really know how to handle all sorts of difficulties, but they simply are unaware that they have this information. We have a great deal of knowledge stored in our unconscious minds which, consciously, we do not know exists. By using the imagination to go into the future when the problem has been solved, we are using a technique which apparently helps us tap into this information.

PROCEDURES

Procedures like this are the second information-gaining tool. They usually involve certain key questions which focus attention on relevant material. One of the more effective of these is the **evidence question**: 'What will you accept as evidence that you have solved the problem?' This relates to the outcome frame, asking how the meeting will know:

(i) when it has identified the reasons why the firm is losing money;
(ii) when it has decided on the appropriate action to be taken to reverse the trend.

Asked early in the proceedings, this question sets up precise criteria which will save a lot of useless discussion.

So, too, will the **difference question**, which asks: 'What is the difference between the time six months ago when we were making profits and today when we are making a loss?' Attention is concentrated upon the key aspect so that the information most relevant to solution of the problem can be drawn forth from the participants.

As solutions are advanced, further procedural questions may be asked. One takes the form of the **efficiency challenge**: 'What facts are known that will eliminate this potential course of action from consideration?' In other words, is this solution workable in the light of the information we have or is there something someone knows which eliminates it as a possibility?

Another useful procedural question is the **relevancy challenge** which puts the question: 'How will this . . . (solution, idea, proposal) achieve what we want? How is it connected with the problem we are working on?' Without challenges of this kind, much decision making time is wasted as meetings are sidetracked by information not really related to the problem at hand. Proposals, ideas, solutions need to be relevant to the issue under discussion and, if the speaker cannot demonstrate the relevance of the point he is making, he must not be permitted to waste the time of the meeting. The efficiency and relevancy challenges provide procedures through which this can be accomplished.

When a dead-end is reached, the **recycling procedure** may be used, perhaps in the form of: 'How else might we use this information to . . .?' There are usually many alternative solutions possible from the same information. If one path of action seems unrewarding, it is often valuable to return to the starting point and consider the data from a different viewpoint, perhaps asking different questions of it to ensure everyone at the meeting shares the same understanding.

POINTERS

This is what pointers, McMaster and Grinder's third set of tools, attempt to do. Whereas frames define the boundaries of exploration through establishing the appropriate context, and procedures are specific ways of maintaining the frames, and of keeping people on the track, pointers are the actual tools for gaining high quality information. They do this by ensuring that everyone understands in the same way what is being said.

The first pointer is the **noun blockbuster**, the 'which' or 'what' question. When a noun is used, as in the statement: 'Well, our *costs* are up', or 'Our *machines* are overpriced', it is challenged. 'What costs are up?', 'Which machines are overpriced?' Unless such challenges are made, people may delude themselves that they are talking about the same thing when in fact they are not.

In the same way, 'how' questions are necessary to make verbs specific. Referred to as the **action blockbuster**, this pointer operates in sentences such as: 'Our margins *are* up' or 'We will *increase* productivity' by asking: 'How much are margins up?' and 'How will you increase production?'

A third tool, the **universal blockbuster**, challenges comments such as: 'I've talked to all the workers and they . . .' and 'Every section is performing to capacity'. It focuses on the use of universals: '*All* the workers?', '*Every* section?' Most of us are far too fond of such sweeping statements. They give a very misleading picture and, by so doing, provide poor quality information upon which to base decisions.

Universals often give too optimistic a view of a situation. On the other hand, statements such as: 'Company policy would not permit us to . . .' and 'We've never done it that way' tend to be too pessimistic. **Boundary crossing** challenges are needed to ensure that the objections really are valid: 'What would happen if Company Policy was different on this point?' or 'What prevents us . . .?' All possibilities for problem solution require exploration and the 'What prevents us from . . .' question is an extremely valuable one. It often makes clear that there is nothing really stopping us at all, only our inner obstacles which say we cannot do something.

A final pointer is the **Comparator**. This is the question: 'Compared to what?', directed against statements such as: 'Our productivity is down' or 'Our labour force is worse now.' As with the other pointers, this question forces the speaker to be specific.

Often problem solutions are not achieved and decisions not made because information is imprecise. Generalities reign supreme. These must be challenged if outcomes are to be achieved. True, the people making such challenges and who demand precision are likely to be rather unpopular. They put the 'wafflers' and the pretentious on the spot. However, they also achieve results in that better decisions are made quickly.

A PROBLEM SOLVING MODEL

In addition to describing tools that may be used to gain information, McMaster and Grinder also outline a specific decision making or problem solving model. It can be shown in this way.

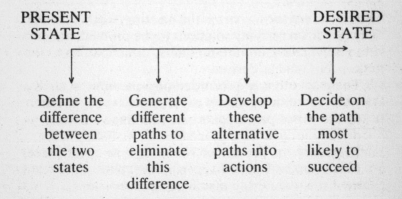

PRESENT STATE ──────────────────────────► DESIRED STATE

| Define the difference between the two states | Generate different paths to eliminate this difference | Develop these alternative paths into actions | Decide on the path most likely to succeed |

By specifying the difference between the Present State, which is what you have now, and the Desired State, which is what you would like to have, you define the problem in concrete terms. The executives of the firm making machine parts had, as their Present State, a loss. As their Desired State, they wanted a profit. So the problem is clearly identified as that of turning losses into profits.

Discussion, aided by the information-gaining tools previously outlined, is directed towards achieving the Desired State, firstly by generating alternative pathways or solutions, then by converting these into concrete actions, and finally by evaluating whether they are likely to succeed in arriving at the desired goal.

These steps embody the brainstorming principle of separating idea generation from idea solution. If ideas are discussed and analyzed immediately they are proposed, they may be killed in their infancy. Therefore, it is desirable to encourage people to provide as many ideas as possible, no matter how peculiar or unorthodox they may be, and then, at a later stage, to ascertain their practicality in the specific situation.

The **Nominal Group** technique for problem solving and decision making makes use of this principle, though in a way somewhat different from that advanced by McMaster and Grinder. In this approach, once the problem has been identified, the following procedure takes place.

1 Executives taking part in the meeting, working alone, write down as many solutions to the problem as come to mind. As there are no limits, these may be as unconventional as desired.

2 These solutions are recorded on a medium, such as a whiteboard or butcher's paper, which is easily visible to the other participants. At this stage, there is no discussion, just a list of ideas.

3 Discussion of the list of solutions now takes place. Much combining and recombining takes place until the list is reduced to manageable proportions.

4 Priorities are then allocated. Each executive records his preferences, arranging the solutions according to how he perceives their worth.
5 Planning is the final step. Those solutions with the highest number of votes are retained for final consideration, a choice of action being made from among them. At times, one alternative will receive overwhelming support. On other occasions, several possibilities while have to be considered before a final solution can be selected.

Both this model and that of McMaster and Grinder are systematic ways of marshalling information to arrive at problem solutions and implement them. Both models stress conscious mental processes, the deliberate focusing of attention to arrive at a rational, reasonable solution.

CONSCIOUS PROBLEM SOLVING

Problem identification is the key to problem solution. Expressed like this, it sounds obvious. And it is. Yet in my experience as a consultant to the business community, as a supervisor of students doing theses, and as a therapist, I have found defining the problem to be the greatest single difficulty involved when decisions have to be made. People continually attempt to solve problems without really knowing what the problems are.

After I've had discussions with clients, they often say: 'That was so helpful. You've clarified my mind for me and now I know what to do'. Yet I may have done very little. In the course of conversation, clients clarify their own thinking, and, by so doing, identify their problems and arrive at solutions. People have the resources within themselves to do this, but often need a little outside help, perhaps in the form of questions which make them think more precisely.

I believe the Present State—Desired State concept to be the most effective way of quickly identifying problems.

Cast in terms of: 'What do you have now?' and 'What do you want to have?', most people immediately see the gap between the two states. This gap is the problem. Attention may then be focused on how to remove this gap.

If the gap is large, perhaps it is necessaary to divide it into sub-problems. Should the problem be present losses as opposed to desired gains, it could be sub-divided into (i) cutting costs, and (ii) increasing sales. Further specification could involve different aspects of cost cutting and sales promotion. However, it is more common to find that the problem identified by the gap between the Present and the Desired States may be handled as it is. Then there are some useful questions you can ask.

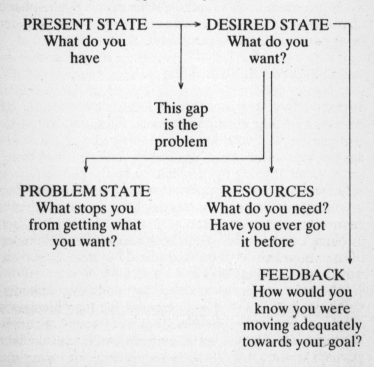

PRESENT STATE ———▸ DESIRED STATE ⌐
What do you   What do you
have   want?

     This gap
     is the
     problem

PROBLEM STATE   RESOURCES
What stops you   What do you need?
from getting what Have you ever got
you want?   it before

         FEEDBACK
         How would you
         know you were
         moving adequately
         towards your goal?

The most useful question to ask, once the problem has been identified, is: 'What prevents you moving from your Present State to your Desired State?' This point was made earlier but the repetition here is deliberate. If you ask yourself this question each time you have defined your problem, and endeavour to answer honestly, you will become, overnight, a vastly improved decision maker.

For example: 'What prevents the firm making profits?' Union trouble? Dissatisfied customers? Outmoded company policy? Overpriced products? Each answer can be analysed using the tools described earlier in this chapter. As this is done, it usually becomes very clear what is stopping a firm or person arriving at the Desired State.

Sometimes, it may be lack of information. If this is so, the situation can be rectified, again using the appropriate tools to ensure the information gained is of sufficient quality to provide a basis for action. However, we often have all the information we need to solve our problem. We just do not realize that we have it.

This is where the 'What prevents you?' questions is so valuable. It cuts through all the excuses, the generalities, the blaming, and makes you look hard at the problem. Perhaps it is you or your firm which needs to change an attitude or a policy. In other words, the question reveals that you are the problem. You are refusing to take action against your inner opponents such as fear, doubt and anxiety.

Similarly, a firm may be its own worst enemy, blaming its difficulties on external factors when, in reality, it is creating its own problems through internal obstacles, such as outmoded attitudes, prejudices which distort incoming information and an unrealistic belief system about the way business 'should' work.

When the problem is defined, and additional information gathered, conscious problem solving then involves a deliberate search for possible solutions. Groups of people may provide more of these than an individual working alone. However, groups often emphasize the safe, the conventional. They tend to reject unusual solutions.

That is why **brainstorming**, which is basically the separation of idea generation from idea evaluation, can be so valuable in a group situation. It works against the group average, the pressure to conform. An 'open' individual, operating alone, may generate many more unusual and workable solutions than a large group, although the less 'open' person will tend to do far worse.

Both the Precision model of McMaster and Grinder, and the Nominal Group technique will help in providing opportunities for many possible solutions to be aired. The key is openness, defined as the ability to suspend judgment while ideas are being produced, to avoid criticism until a later stage when evaluation is necessary.

Once the 'best' solution is decided upon, this is put into effect as quickly as possible. A measure of performance needs to be agreed upon at the same time so that its success may be evaluated. The question: 'What evidence will I accept that this action has solved the problem?' is a valuable one at this stage in that it establishes a definite criterion. If the solution meets this criterion, it is retained as successful. If not, the recycling procedure takes place and an alternative solution is put into operation. This is a logical, reasonable process, but logic and reason are only part of successful decision making and problem solving.

UNCONSCIOUS PROBLEM SOLVING

John McAllister is the general manager of the machine parts firm described in this chapter. For some time before he called the meeting of his executives, John was aware of the problem the firm faced. He knew, if the firm was to survive, profits had to be increased, so he explored several possibilities. Staff could be reduced, certain production operations streamlined, some marginally profitable lines eliminated, sales techniques improved.

Quite consciously, John defined the problem, reviewed the salient facts he had at his disposal, and thought about possible solutions. These he jotted down on paper. However, he made no attempt to arrive at a 'best' answer. He realized that his conscious mind had access to very limited information and, by employing the vast resources of his unconscious mind, he could improve his chance of arriving at an effective solution to his problem.

Accordingly, John 'primed' his unconscious mind, focusing it on the problem at hand by feeding in the information he had available. Then he turned his conscious mind away from this problem by doing something quite different. This could have been some other work matter but John had found, through previous experience, that a relaxation period was more likely to leave the unconscious mind free to solve the problem in its own way.

Sometimes, depending on the time of day, John would leave his office and, at a nearby health club, either go for a swim or do some weight training. Should circumstances be such that he was unable to leave the premises, John would move away from his desk to a corner of his office which he had set up as a relaxation area. He never used this area for work. Instead, stretching out in an easy chair, he would read some light fiction or listen to music which suited his mood.

Usually, after he had spent some time relaxing in this way, John would return to his desk with new material to add to his 'priming' outline. In this particular case, he found he had little to add to his first ideas, so he put away the sheet of paper. On his calendar, he made a note to look at this paper on increasing profits later in the afternoon, then occupied himself with other work.

On previous occasions, fifteen to twenty minutes had proven sufficient time to 'let' the ideas flow. That is the secret of using unconscious mental processes for decision making. It is necessary to 'let it happen'. You cannot force the process. The more you try to do so, the less effective this approach becomes. Once you've consciously 'primed' your mind and turned the problem over to the unconscious, allow it to proceed in its own way without interference. In other words, trust your unconscious.

Later in the afternoon, when John returned to consider his first jottings on how profits might be increased, several

PROBLEM SOLVING

Conscious

- What is the problem? (define it)
- Is it too big to handle? (sub-divide it)
- What information do I have?
- What additional information do I need?
- What are the possible solutions?
- What is the 'best' solution?
- Did the solution work? (if not try another)

Subconscious

- Prime the mind consciously with:
  - ◆ definite problem
  - ◆ review of pertinent facts
  - ◆ possible solutions
- Turn it over to the subconscious for solution:
  - ◆ let it happen
  - ◆ use a reminder
  - ◆ before sleeping, sport, hobby, relaxation

ideas came into his mind which had not occurred to him previously. These he noted and, when nothing further was forthcoming, put the paper away, making a calendar entry to look at it again the next day.

He continued in this way for several days, always finding there was something more to add. In addition, he used the periods before going to sleep and before playing golf, which he did every weekend, to quickly review the problem. This was not done with any sense of worry or urgency. Rather, it was a quiet checking over the state of progress.

John had his solution in six days. Actually, most of it was available after the third day, but he had learned from past experience to allow plenty of time for the unconscious development of ideas. Several quite useful variants 'popped' into his mind over the next few days until the solution emerged in complete form. John took this solution to the meeting, not advancing it until the other participants had expressed their own ideas. In this way he was able to check his unconsciously-derived formulation against the conscious problem solving efforts of his associates.

Use of the unconscious mind in this way is really just commonsense. We have this marvellous equipment for problem solving and decision making, yet so often we do not use it. At least, we do not use it systematically. It will provide us with the answers we need if we allow it to do so, saving us a lot of time in the process for it is working while we are doing other things.

THE IMAGINATION AND THE UNCONSCIOUS

There are a number of problem solving techniques using unconscious mental processes which may be triggered through the imagination. Many may be found in Jose Silva's book, *The Silva Mind Control Method for Business Managers*, although, in one form or another, they are present in a number of systems which make use of the unconscious to solve problems. A variant on one of these, the Mirror of the Mind, is set out below.

1 Either lying or sitting down, breathe deeply and slowly, allowing relaxation to occur at its own rate. This process, which has been present in most of the imaginative exercises used in this book, is often described as going to the Alpha level. All this means is that when we relax, our brain waves assume a slower rhythm than in our alert state.
2 Imagine that you have a Mental Screen in your mind, possibly in the third eye position at the base of the nose.
3 Create a visualization of your problem, and project this onto your Mental Screen, around which you have placed a blue frame. Study the problem.

4 Wipe the problem from the Screen. Change the colour of the frame from blue to white, and visualize how things will be when you have solved your problem. This could be in the form of a goal image or a solution.

5 Whenever, in the future, you think about that problem, always 'see' your goal image framed in white.

Another very useful technique has similarities to the Inner Advisor technique described in the previous chapter.

IMAGINARY CONSULTANT

● Before going to sleep, enter the Alpha state. As you visualize a problem situation, such as selling a property, invite an imaginary consultant to enter the picture you have mentally created. This person should be somebody whose expertise in the problem area you respect.

● Instruct yourself to awaken at that time during the night or early morning which will be best for you to work on your problem, then fall asleep. By giving yourself such an instruction while you are in the Alpha state of relaxation, you programme your subconscious mind to do your bidding.

● When you awaken during the night, breathe deeply and relax to enter the Alpha state. Welcome your imaginary consultant. In your mind, 'see' the property and ask the first question that needs to be decided (for example 'Shall I sell privately or use an estate agent?').

● Pair the two choices, ask your consultant which is best, switch away to other thoughts, then come back again and the answer should be in your mind.

● Continue to pair choices pertaining to your problem, switch thoughts, return, and get your answers.

● Thank your imaginary consultant and fall asleep again.

This can be used in any situation when faced with alternatives. Take a few deep breaths, relax as you let go your breath, unfocus your eyes, imagine an expert beside you, pair alternatives, and get your answer as to which of these is best. It is certainly very helpful to have such imaginary consultants to call upon when needed. We also need to be able to work successfully with real people, that being the subject of the next chapter.

10 Working With Others

ESTABLISHING RAPPORT

As you work with other people, either as collegue, manager, or subordinate, you will find there are three keys to success. The first of these is to establish rapport, and the most important aspect of getting on someone else's wave length is to **pace first, then lead**. This means that before we can influence someone else to do what we want, we have first to understand his or her view of the world.

Although rapport may be defined in many ways, we shall consider it in terms of sharing other people's view of the world. This does not mean that we must agree with everything that others believe, only that we can demonstate an understanding of those beliefs. If we are able to transmit this understanding, others feel as if we are 'on their wavelength', able to see things from their point of view. In this way, rapport is created and, once this pacing of others' beliefs has been achieved, it becomes possible to lead them towards differing viewpoints. Perhaps an example might make this concept clearer.

In my work as a therapist, I often encounter patients with stories which seem somewhat unusual. This was true of Eva Voight. This woman consulted me because: 'All my neighbours hate me. I'm really a good person but, when someone new comes into the neighbourhood, the others turn her against me. They even follow me when I go shopping and spy on me.'

It would be very easy to argue with a story like this,

suggesting that the woman was exaggerating. Yet, if I did behave in this way, any chance of my helping her would be lost. No one likes to be doubted. Besides, she may be right. All her neighbours may actually hate her and spy on her. I don't know, and I would be very arrogant if I acted as if she was wrong and didn't know what she was talking about.

It is so easy to act like this, though. Look at your own behaviour. How often do you tell someone they are wrong because what they are saying doesn't agree with your own beliefs? This is all right if what you want is an argument but, if you wish to influence somebody, to have them do whatever it is that you desire, such an approach is doomed to failure.

An approach that offers far more chance of success is, initially, to share the other person's view of the world. I sympathized with Eva, agreeing that it would be very difficult living in such circumstances, particularly when there seemed no reason for her neighbours to behave in such a way.

Eva responded favourably to my pacing, in that a comfortable rapport was established. Once she satisfied herself that I was able to see things in the same way as she did, she decided I could be trusted. Then I could lead her to a different viewpoint, one likely to improve the quality of her life. This I did through the use of statements emphasizing the doubtful aspects of her view: 'And to think that *all* your neighbours behave like this, *every one* of them.'

Eva then modified her original story. Perhaps not every one of her neighbours hated her. In fact, it came down to only three who behaved badly towards her. But note that it was Eva who made this change. It was not I who suggested it was unlikely that all her neighbours hated her.

Continuing this line of leading, I focused on the spying difficulty with statements like: 'I would hate it if I was followed *every* time I went shopping. That would be very upsetting, being followed on *every single occasion*.'

Again, Eva modified her story. It appeared that it had only happened once, and even then she had some doubts about whether it actually was the car of one of her neighbours.

Although this example might seem extreme, it isn't. In one form or another, most people, including the people with whom we work, adopt unrealistic beliefs. Yet to meet such beliefs head on, pointing out how wrong they are, is usually a waste of time. Worse, actually, because when our beliefs are challenged, we feel impelled to support them even more strongly.

Pacing and leading are incredibly powerful techniques for establishing rapport. Once you have done so, you will be able to exert a great influence over others. After all, it is at the basis of **3F**, one of the oldest and most effective sales techniques in the world.

(i)   The first F involves finding out, through listening and asking questions, how the *other person feels*.

(ii) The second F reassures the person that many *others have felt* the same way. It is amazing how often people think they are the only ones with a problem. By telling them about others with the same difficulty you help them feel a lot better.

(iii) The third F involves stories and examples demonstrating how these other people *found* that by doing whatever it is that you are suggesting, they were able to meet their needs, or solve their problem.

In this way you can sell products, ideas, and yourself very successfully. Whatever we do, most of the time we are selling in one form or another. This technique in a way of ensuring that we sell effectively.

The beauty of such pacing and leading techniques is that, hopefully, both you and your 'customer' get what you want. It is a win-win situation. Obviously it could be used to manipulate others into doing things against their best interests. Like other methods and techniques described in this book, it is a tool which is capable of being used either to help or to harm others. I hope readers will opt for the former as it is not only more humane, it also pays off in creating a pleasant working environment.

Others ways of creating the rapport which generates such an environment include **asking questions which generate 'yes' answers** quickly. If you are able to get someone saying 'Yes', 'Yes', 'Yes' to your initial inquiries, it is usually relatively easy to keep him or her on this positive track so that, when you come to the important issues, your chances of agreement are very high.

Probably the easiest way of getting these 'Yes' responses is to take something the other person has said and turn it into a question. If he has mentioned that he is an engineer, a little later in the conversation you might say: "You said that you are an engineer didn't you?" or "Engineering is your line of work isn't it?" This establishes the 'Yes' set rather than the 'No' set.

Psychologists have found that when people respond to questionnaires they tend to answer later questions in the same way as the early ones. If they begin with 'Yes', many of them keep on responding in this way. Should they begin with 'No', they will tend to stay with that answer. Therefore, when attempting to establish rapport, avoid questions which are likely to elicit a 'No', particularly early in the contact. That is why it is so counter-productive to tell people they are wrong or mistaken when they tell you something with which you do not agree, or which appears strange to you. Save the benefit of your superior knowledge until after you have established a rapport.

Expressing warmth will help you do so, for we usually feel good about people who show liking for us. By smiling, keeping eye contact and using the other person's name whenever appropriate, you convey this feeling of warmth. Showing interest in what he or she is saying, prompting further conversation with questions, and listening attentively consolidate this rapport.

During the early stages of contact, **avoid arguments**. In fact, unless you feel the need to wrangle, it is not a bad idea to avoid arguments as much as possible. As salesmen have been told so often, the customer is never wrong. When you are attempting to persuade others to do as you want, adopt this principle. It will bring you far more success than meeting head on in an argument. You may win the argument, but, even if you do get what you want from the other person on this occasion, it will be much harder next time. On the other hand, if you take the time to use the more subtle approach in achieving rapport, it becomes easier and easier to work with other people.

At times it is very difficult to agree with what someone else is saying if it violates a dearly held belief or principle. That is understandable. To overcome this difficulty while still building rapport, sympathize by saying: '**If I was in your situation I would feel just the same**'. That is probably quite true, and by speaking in this way you encourage the other person to feel that you understand his or her situation. It is that feeling which is the essence of rapport.

MAKING THE OTHER PERSON FEEL IMPORTANT

This is the second key to success. It has been said that from the cradle to the grave, life is a search for importance. All of us like to think that we matter in some way. The American humourist Will Rogers once said that we are all ignorant, but about different things. The same might be said for insecurity. We are all insecure, but about different things. Thus, **we all need 'strokes'** to help us feel better, more secure about ourselves and our own worth.

Some years ago, Art Buchwald, writing in the *Washington Post*, told a little story that points this up quite well. He and a friend were travelling across mid-town Manhattan in a cab. At the end of the trip, as Buchwald paid the cabbie, he congratulated him on the way he had handled the peak hour traffic. His friend inquired why he had bothered as the cabbie didn't seem too impressed. Buch-wald's reply was that he intended to change the face of New York by saying or doing something each day that would make ten people feel better. Because of the 'lift' they received, these people, in turn, would be more pleasant to others, so it would be like throwing a stone into a pond with the ripples spreading out in all directions.

As they walked along a street, Buchwald and his friend stopped to chat to some bricklayers taking their coffee break. He admired the building on which they were work-ing, commenting that they must feel considerable pride in contributing to such a fine looking edifice. A couple of the men ignored him but others responded positively, obviously pleased someone had recognized the value of their work.

We like and need 'strokes', positive things that make us feel better. Interestingly enough, half a dozen people de-liberately setting out each day to say or do positive things are able to change the climate of large organizations. So, too, are those who do the opposite, constantly criticising and complaining.

We all know of people who seem to walk around im-mersed in a black cloud, exerting a negative influence on everyone they meet. They do not make us feel important, as if we matter. Quite the contrary. Such people con-tribute nothing to workplace harmony, whereas the Buchwald approach does much to make working with others a very enjoyable experience.

This is because we are very susceptible to suggestions from other people, a phenomenon brought out very strongly in a seminar I conducted for medical students. A week before the seminar, I organized three students to follow the Buchwald pattern by offering at least five 'strokes' every day to their collegues. Three other stu-dents were to do the opposite, offering at least five nega-tive comments to those with whom they came into contact.

As I began the seminar, I told the medical students

what had been going on the previous week. From the back
of the room came an anguished wail. One unfortunate
character had had the bad luck to meet the three 'negative' students one after the other. He had arrived at university one morning, feeling quite all right. However,
after being told by three different people that he looked
ill, needed more sleep, and had aged overnight, this stu-
dent went home to bed, convinced he was sick.

Such is the power of suggestion. Other students related
how their low moods had been transformed through the
'strokes' they received. The process is so simple, so easy
to put into operation , and the favourable results are out
of all proportion to the amount of effort expended. The
Buchwald approach must surely be one of the most important ways of creating harmony in human relationships. It
is really a mystery why we use it so rarely.

Praise, perhaps the most effective of 'strokes' is so important. If there be one rule for successful management it
is to **catch people doing something right and praise them**
for it. Yet, we usually do the reverse. When others are
doing what we want them to do, we ignore them. Should
they do something wrong though, we come down on them
like a ton of bricks. This is true of the way we bring up our
children, it is typical of how schools operate, and is particularly characteristic of the functioning of government
bureaucracies.

By catching people doing something right and praising
them, you help them to feel important. Perhaps, instead
of praising them directly, you may **work through a third
person**. Dennis Taylor is a hotel manager who uses this
approach a lot. When Dennis knows that two of his
employees are very friendly, he will often praise one of
them to the other, feeling confident that his praise will
be passed on. Often the indirectness of this 'stroke'
makes it easier for the recipient to accept.

There are a number of other techniques that Dennis
uses to help his employees feel a sense of worth. He will
often **ask for advice, opinions, favours, and solutions**. By

doing so he is saying that others have skills, knowledge and abilities which he values. Showing his appreciation of the work they do is his way of giving a dog a good rather than a bad name. We tend to get what we expect and, by his behaviour, Dennis makes clear that he has positive expectations of his staff.

He is also **sparing with criticism**. When it is required, Dennis always begins with something positive, then gets to the criticism, and ends with another positive aspect. In this way, he maximizes the chances that the person being criticized will actually do something about his failing. Rushing in headlong with a spate of complaints is unlikely to effect change because the recipient is swamped. However, if he has only one thing upon which to concentrate, and this is presented along with praise, the chances are that the change will be made. As ill-feeling is minimized, the harmony of the work situation is maintained.

IDENTIFY THE OTHER PERSON'S DOMINANT INTEREST

Many years ago, Dale Carnegie in *How to Win Friends and Influence People*, identified the third key to success in working with others when he made the point that it is important to **listen rather than talk**. When we listen and question, we are usually able to identify other people's dominant desires. We can then use this information to show others how to get what they want by doing the things we suggest. The Americans call this hitting the 'hot button'. By constantly making reference to this dominant interest, and linking it to our own purpose, we are usually able to create another of those win-win situations where everyone is happy.

However, to be successful in this approach, we do need to be good listeners. Such people display most of the following characteristics.

GOOD LISTENERS

- Listen without talking.
- Listen for speaker's main ideas.
- Are aware of prejudices, emotional deaf spots, which cause their minds to go off on tangents.
- Fight off distractions such as noise, speaker's mannerisms.
- Avoid anger which interferes with clear message reception.
- Take brief notes when the material they receive is important.
- Allow the other person to tell his or her story first, then make their own contribution.
- Empathize by seeing the other person's point of view.
- Withhold judgement.
- React to the message, not to the person giving it.
- Recognize the emotion behind the speaker's words rather than the literal meaning.
- Use feedback to check their understanding of what has been said, telling the other person what they thought he or she meant.
- Create a relaxed environment.
- Withhold criticism of a viewpoint different from their own.
- Listen attentively, using eye contact and verbal encouragement.
- Ask open-ended questions allowing the other person to express his or her feelings and thoughts.
- Are motivated to listen because attitude is vital.

Unfortunately, most of us do not listen in this way. We are more likely to evaluate and judge what someone else is saying so that we can plan a critical answer, expressing our superiority by contradictions. In this way, we behave as if we are engaged in some competition with the other person, having to demonstrate that what he or she is saying is of less value than what we have to say.

Jumping to conclusions before the speaker has finished what he or she is saying is also something most of us do, assuming that everyone else thinks the same way as ourselves. As a matter of course, we tend to tune out people with whom we do not agree, or else hear what we want or expect to hear rather than what is actually being said. When our beliefs are challenged we often do not listen at all.

As if that litany of listening sins is not enough, we also tend to let our minds wander and our attention stray. Accordingly, we fail to clarify what others mean by the particular words they choose. In the last chapter when I talked about the information gaining tools, the necessity of such clarification of other peoples' words became apparent.

Another reason why we do not spend time in such clarification is that we are too busy either preparing to speak ourselves, or actually speaking. Many people do talk excessively, dominating the conversation so that others have little opportunity to express themselves adequately.

Emerson was once moved to comment: 'Better to remain silent and be thought a fool than to speak up and remove all doubt'. On another occasion he said, somewhat caustically: 'No one ever learns anything while their own mouths are open'. Perhaps such comments are a little extreme but, if you observe people who are influential, they rarely suffer from verbal diarrhoea. Instead, they tend to wait patiently while others do most of the talking and then, choosing their time, come in quietly and firmly with a briefly worded opinion or suggestion which is usually accepted. Such people are most effective as negotiators.

LIFE'S ENCOUNTERS AS NEGOTIATIONS

George O'Neill, who manages a drug company, is such a man. A skilled negotiator, he has applied, to his life in general, principles which have worked well for him in his business dealings. He concentrates on essentials, not allowing himself to get enmeshed in detail. Adept at instant compromises which clinch deals, he realizes that most people will settle on some positive outcome, even if it does not satisfy them completely, rather than write off hours of negotiation as a waste of time. Taking a lead from Cohen's book, *You Can Negotiate Anything*, he sees **life's events as a series of negotiations**, believing that it is possible to get most of the things he wants by using the following basic principles.

NEGOTIATING PRINCIPLES

Treat negotiation as a game in that nothing can annoy you without your consent. Detach yourself and enjoy it.

- Never eliminate an option without getting something in return.
- Always test your assumptions—things are not as they are but as we are.
- Believe and act 'as if' you have the power to influence others.
- Instead of showing how clever you are, begin gently, seeking help and asking questions to emphasize common needs and goals.
- Find out what the other person really wants and show him or her a way of getting it while you also get what you want.
- Use the power of legitimacy, the printed word when it is to your advantage, but challenge it when it is not.
- Use the power of precedent for your own advantage—but question it when used against you.
- Challenge an expert with irreverance, innocence, questions. Establish your own expertise by careful preparation, to-the-point questions, and use of suitable jargon.
- Convey a positive expectancy of the other person's honesty and good will—give him or her a good reputation.

- Never care so much that you MUST have something.
- Attempt to see things from the other person's viewpoint—listen attentively.
- Allow the other person to 'save face' by not embarrassing him or her publicly.
- Instead of: 'You are confusing me,' say: 'I feel confused by what you are saying.'—replace 'you' with 'I'.

These principles have wide applicability because they usually achieve the results desired by their user. To be successful, then, we must learn to use the skills of negotiation, and this is primarily a matter of knowing how to communicate effectively.

11 Successful Communication

COMMUNICATION—EFFECTIVE AND INEFFECTIVE

The essence of effective communication is that the receiver of a message understands it in the way the sender intended. Diagrammatically, it looks like this:

When communication is ineffective, the diagram includes an additional element:

In this case, the receiver understands the the sender's message differently from the way it was intended.

To decide if a particular communication has been effective or ineffective, check the receiver's understanding. It is not a question of the sender's intent, but whether the receiver actually grasped the message in the way it was meant. A foreman can explain, to a man on the production line, carefully, slowly and thoroughly exactly how he wants a car part assembled. If the man assembles it incorrectly, he has not understood the explanation. The foreman has not communicated successfully.

Many things interfere with communication. Some of these are a function of the way senders transmit their messages. Perhaps they talk too quickly, or use words with which the receiver is unfamiliar, or have annoying mannerisms which distract listeners. Maybe they are uncertain of the material they wish to communicate, and, because of this, present it in a confusing manner.

Although such behaviour complicates the task of the receiver, it is not the basic reason why so many messages are misunderstood. The fault usually lies with the receiver. Why? He or she simply does not listen. Probably this is what happened with the production line man who misunderstood the instructions of his foreman. He got it wrong because he wasn't listening.

As pointed out in the last chapter, listening is something most of us find difficult. Really listening, that is. Usually we are too occupied thinking of what we intend to say next, thus we pay little attention to what the other person is saying. Because of our inattention, we misunderstand the message and our reply is inappropriate. We've probably all had the experience of sharing a conversation in which people believed they were all talking about the same thing but were, in fact, going off in quite different directions.

After all, if the receiver of a communication is really listening, he can actually make the sender give a clear message. He does so by asking questions to clarify aspects he does not understand. To ensure that he knows precisely how the sender is defining the words he is using, the good listener asks: 'What do you mean by. . .?', and 'Give me an example of. . .'. He can also request that the speaker slow down, repeat statements, and speak more clearly so that he gets the message clearly.

If a receiver behaves in this way, it shows not only that he or she is actively listening, but it also forces the sender to communicate clearly. He or she cannot simply rattle off a message and, if the receiver does not understand it, say 'Well, it's his funeral. I told him what to do,' which is an all-too-common attitude. Unfortunately, however, it is relatively uncommon for receivers to behave in this way.

For this, there is one main reason. A human being may be seen as a transmitter which sends signals, as a receiver which accepts signals, and, also, as a record player. In our minds we have many 'records'—memories of past experiences—and when a word or two, spoken by someone sending a message, triggers one of these memories, the appropriate 'record' drops onto the turntable and starts playing. Once this happens, we no longer pay any attention to the incoming message. Our attention is elsewhere, occupied by the 'record' playing our mind. That is what we are listening to, and it usually interferes with the sender's message so powerfully that we do not understand it. How can we? We are simply not listening because we are so engrossed in our 'record'.

THE RECORDS WE PLAY

There are many, many 'records' we play on our mental turntables which interfere with successful reception of communication directed towards us. Many of these are very pleasant. Perhaps we are chatting with a business associate who happens to mention, say, Fiji or Hawaii. The very name sparks memories of a marvellous holiday we have spent at one of those places, and our mind drifts off to relive these. Our acquaintance talks on without realizing he or she no longer has an audience.

Similarly, pleasant 'records' of good times with the

family, a successful business deal, a great game of golf, may be triggered off by a word or two spoken incidentally, not really related to the matter under discussion. However, as our minds become immersed in the happy experiences summoned up by these words, we miss the import of the communication.

Some 'records', however, are not so pleasant. **Worry** is one of these. A word invokes a disturbing memory and, from that point, the other person may just as well be talking to a brick wall. Your 'worry record' has got you.

Jillian Kirby, who manages the women's clothing department of a large store, was listening to one of her saleswomen tell her about a very difficult customer. In the course of the conversation, the saleswoman mentioned that this women, overweight as she was, insisted on squeezing into a small woman's fitting. The word 'weight' triggered one of Jillian's 'worry records', for she seemed always to be engaged in a losing battle against excessweight. The 'record' continued playing as she considered whether she could miss lunch, or perhaps have only a salad at dinner time. Of course, nothing further the saleswoman said registered with Jillian for, mentally, she was no longer present.

Most of us are plagued by worries, fears, doubts, anxieties, and guilts (the Inner Game obstacles referred to earlier) which prevent us realizing our full potential as human beings. It is these obstacles which are particularly disruptive of effective communication for they provide the most compelling of all 'records', the ones which so completely absorb our attention that we cannot listen to what others are saying.

Jillian is caught, for worry over her weight intrudes constantly. All it takes is a word, or the sight of an overweight woman, to turn her inward, oblivious of the outside world. How can she turn off this worrying? How can she lift the 'record' from the turntable so she can attend to what others are saying?

In an earlier chapter, I suggested that interruption is the

answer. She needs to deliberately direct her attention away from the internal 'worry record' to something else. Worry is a habit, one at which we become expert through constant practice. As long as Jillian allows herself to continue worrying, she becomes better and better at it. The habit grows increasingly strong. However, by deliberately interrupting herself each time she realizes she is worrying, Jillian introduces a competing habit. As she practices this, it eventually becomes more powerful than the original habit so that, if she starts to worry, the new habit unconsciously triggers an interruption which directs her attention elsewhere.

Jillian could also use the techniques of action meditation, of concentrating intently on the person to whom she is talking, noticing how her lips move as she speaks, how quickly or slowly she talks, and whether she gestures. Or she could devote her complete attention to the other person's words, becoming an active listener by asking questions, smiling, and showing her interest through the non-verbal language of body position.

By concentrating her energies outwardly rather than inwardly, Jillian not only could switch her attention away from her 'worry records', but also ensure she will facilitate the communication process.

She could also practise detachment, letting the worrying thought drift through her mind without making any attempt to actively pursue it. To facilitate this, Jillian might like to think of her mind as a room with two windows, one on either side of her head. Should a worrying thought occur, she can choose to observe it in a detached way, then allow it to float across her mind out of the other window.

Using this method, Jillian can train herself to let the thousands of thoughts which come to her during the day drift in one window and out the other. Should a pleasing, productive or creative thought come along, she can, mentally, shut the windows to keep it in her mind. It then becomes *her* thought. Until this point, it is only *a* thought.

'Easier said than done' has been the comment I have often heard when recommending this approach. Yet, is it? How often have you gone to a room in your house to get something and, by the time you have got there, forgotten what it was you wanted? Unless we make a real effort to retain them, thoughts float in and out of our minds effortlessly. If this happens so naturally, it means we must be making some sort of effort to keep the worrying thoughts in our minds, and that is crazy. We can let go of these just as we let go of the non-worrying ones.

THE CRITICISM RECORD

This 'record' ranks second only to worry as a source of interference to the communication process. When we are talking with others, someone may say something which we construe as critical. Our 'criticism record' drops onto the turntable and, in most cases, we react mechanically, defending ourselves by verbally attacking the other person. Under these circumstances we behave more like machines than human beings, reacting to the 'how dare anyone criticize me' tune that is being played in our minds. When this occurs, any hope of effective communication is lost.

Gary Swenson, a buyer for a chain of menswear stores, is controlled by his 'criticism record'. The most innocent remarks of others start the record spinning. As a result, Gary communicates badly, his listening process disrupted by the internal message: 'How dare he or she say that that to me'. Naturally enough, people find Gary touchy, and this has adversely affected his career. A pity, for he has a marvellous flair for buying clothes which sell well.

The retail chain for which he works values this ability but refuses to promote him because, instead of listening to what people want, he fights them. Remedies mentioned in the chapter on health, such as Impatiens and Nux Vomica, would help him, as would a change of attitude.

To remove the 'criticism record' from the turntable of his mind, Gary could choose to respond only to actual words spoken, and to ignore the implications which he reads into those words. A superior says: 'Gary, I can't seem to find your report on your last buying trip to America'. Gary's usual response would be something along the lines: 'Of course I wrote the report. You had it on your desk three days after I got back. I always make a point of getting those reports out quickly.'

Because he feels he is being criticised for not writing his report, Gary defends himself vehemently. He is listening to his 'criticism record', failing to notice that his superior is speaking in a quiet, friendly way with no trace of aggression. However, Gary's defensive response may well spark a more antagnostic rejoinder from his superior.

All Gary need say is that the report was submitted on a certain date. Should it have gone astray, he can offer to provide a duplicate. That is what Gary's superior wants to know, and it is all that is required. Instead of reading into words implications which may not be present at all, Gary can take them at face value and respond quietly. This would certainly facilitate communication.

So, too, would Gary's recognition that he is human. Human beings make mistakes—constantly. If a criticism is made of us, there is an excellent chance that in it some element of truth is contained. We can choose to accept this and, instead of defending ourselves or attacking the other person, say something like: 'I'm sorry about the report. I've been a bit slow in getting it done. I'll have it for you Monday morning, first thing.'

This is an appropriate reply if the superior is voicing a criticism and Gary has not done the report. Interestingly enough, admitting error and agreeing with the person who is offering the complaint usually turns off criticism very quickly.

Other disruptive 'records' involve negative emotions such as **envy, dislike, resentment and jealousy** which may be triggered quite innocently during discussion. As with worry and criticism, such 'records' absorb our attention leaving little to facilitate communication.

The same is true if we possess **rigid belief systems**. If we firmly believe that people 'should' behave in certain ways, 'ought' to do the things we think are fitting, 'must' come up to our expectation, violations of these beliefs will turn us inward. While we are occupied with 'tut-tutting' about someone else who is not behaving as we think they should, we fail to hear what he or she is saying.

To ensure successful communication, then, learn to turn off the 'records' so you are left free to actually listen to what is being said. This is the key to the communication process, just as it is the key to persuading others to do what you want.

PERSUASIVE COMMUNICATION

Too often, we provide solutions to other people's problems without checking to find if they really have those problems. Looking in from the outside, we do not have much idea of what other people consider as important to them. The only way we can find out is to listen. That is why I have stressed this point so often. To influence others, we need to know what they want, what their dominant desires are, and to then demonstrate that we can help them achieve these.

We might assume that all businessmen and women are motivated by money. That is, their dominant desire is to make a fortune. If the particular businessman to whom we are trying to sell a computer is motivated in this way, we have a good chance of making a sale by showing him that our product will help him make more money. However, if his dominant desire is to be seen as an 'elder statesman' of the industry or to gain more executive power, our appeal to his money-making instinct is likely to be less successful.

I have previously referred to people's dominant desires as their Hot Buttons. To sell them anything, it is largely a matter of constantly hitting their Hot Button during the sales presentation, showing them that they can achieve the things they want most through the use of your product.

Though this technique is usually employed in selling a concrete product, it is just as effective when we are selling ourselves or selling our ideas. That is why it is sometimes necessary to let a person believe that the idea you have implanted in his mind is his own. This is because his dominant desire is for a sense of importance. Should you insist on claiming the idea as your own, he will do nothing about it, probably saying that it is unsound. Let him own it, and suddenly it becomes a wonderful idea.

Most of the time, people are thinking and talking about themselves. Therefore, to identify a person's Hot Button, all you need to do is to listen while he or she talks. If he or she talks but little, use questions until you find out what the dominant desire is, then by showing how you can help in the achievement of this, your communication becomes overwhelmingly persuasive, virtually irresistible. Once needs are identified, a few basic rules you might like to use will increase the power of your communication. These hold whether your audience is one person or a hundred.

- Be simple.
- Use language that is familiar to your audience.
- Tell stories and give examples.

Stories are of great value as a means of giving indirect suggestions. Consider the case of Bill Pearson, an accounts executive in a printing firm, who became very worried over the increasing sleepiness he was experiencing. As a younger man, he was able to work an eight to ten hour hour day without any signs of drowsiness. Now, in his early forties, Bill found himself often struggling against an almost overpowering drowsiness.

With Bill, I used the 3F technique described earlier, for it provides a very powerful means of persuasion. By sharing his consternation over his drowsiness, I accepted and supported Bill's feelings. Then, moving on to the second F, I pointed out that others, including myself, often felt the same way. Finally, the third F, I told stories about these others who had found a solution by taking a short nap or period of quiet meditation during the day.

I quoted examples of executives I knew who hung up a 'Do not disturb' notice on their doors for ten, fifteen or twenty minutes while they simply answered their bodies' need for rest. The result was improved performance. They accomplished more work because their bodies felt refreshed, no longer having to wage a battle against drowsiness. Often this nap or meditation was taken at lunch time, enabling the executives to face the afternoon fresh and alert, as if starting the day anew.

While telling stories or quoting examples, it is possible to embed commands which are not recognized as such by your listeners. As I talked to Bill, for instance, I told him a story about a bank manager who, wanting a nap during his lunch break, took his car down to a quiet place near a beach where he would be undisturbed. During the course of this tale, I said: 'The bank manager found he could sleep for ten minutes and then remain fresh and active for the rest of the day, working better than ever. Lots of people have found the same thing, that *you can increase your working efficiency by taking a short nap.*' I stressed the italicized words with a change in tone so they became an instruction to Bill to take a nap and improve his performance.

Such commands embedded in a more general communication are usually very effective because they are indirect. That is why the telephone can be so valuable in giving advice, though it is most effective when not used in the normal way. If you want to persuade somebody, let's call him Sean, to accept certain advice, arrange for him to come into your office while you are on the phone.

Actually, you either arrange for your secretary to ring you at a certain time when you know Sean will be in your office, or you pretend you are engaged in a telephone conversation when he comes in. Apologize that you cannot give him your full attention for a minute or two until you complete your phone call, then give the non-existent per-

son (for your secretary hangs up as soon as you answer) at
the other end of the line the advice you want Sean to act
upon.

Although you are not talking directly to him, Sean cannot help but overhear what you are saying and is more
likely to act upon what he has heard than if you had told
him directly. It seems that most of us don't like to be told
what to do, yet are more than willing to act upon advice
which we seem to generate for ourselves. The fake telephone conversations plants a seed which is likely to ger-
minate into the flower you want.

Another pattern of persuasive communication involves
these steps.

- Present the problem, usually identified as the gap be-
  tween your Present State (what you have) and your
  Desired State (what you want).
- Offer the solution.
- Prove your case with stories, examples, quotations
  from famous people.
- Appeal for immediate action.

In this above pattern, note that the problem is one that is
being experienced by your audience, not one you think
they might have.

All these ideas are quite straightforward. Whenever
you want to persuade others, try them. You'll find the results very gratifying. As you do use these methods, keep
three points in mind.

- Find out what the other person wants, and help him
  or her achieve it.
- Make your listeners feel important.
- Tell your listeners what they would like to be true
  about themselves.

If you do these three things, you will be a successful com-
municator.

It is not difficult to put these principles into practice. It is unfortunate that successful communication is a skill which manifests itself all too rarely in meetings. Because meetings loom so large in the activities of many firms, however, it seems appropriate that we devote to this ubiquitous aspect of business life a chapter all of its own.

12 Meetings That Satisfy

TO MEET OR NOT TO MEET

In the business world, perhaps no ritual is so severely and frequently criticized as meetings, those 'tribal' gatherings where a number of highly paid executives sit around a table to discuss progress, problems, future directions, and other similar topics. It is rare if these same executives emerge from the meeting with a sense of accomplishment, of having used their time well. Rather, a sense of frustration prevails over time used to little effect.

In *The Efficient Executive*, a book which has now become somewhat of a classic, Peter Drucker wrote:

> 'Another time waster is malorganization. Its symptom is an excess of meetings. Meetings are by definition a concession to deficient organization. For one either meets or works. One cannot do both at the same time. . . . If executives spend more than a fairly small part of their time in meeting, it is a sure sign of malorganization.'

As Drucker goes on to point out, every meeting spawns a host of little follow-up meetings which occupy many hours. Therefore, he argues that, for an organization to be efficient, meetings should be the exception rather than the rule. They should never be allowed to become an executive's main activity.

Despite such a negative view of meetings, there are occasions when one is effective, in that problems are solved, precise action is taken, and a sense of accomplishment is engendered. Meetings fail not because of their inherent nature but because of the way in which they are conducted.

To a great extent, the conduct of a meeting is the responsibility of the person chairing it. However, it is possible for participants other than the chairman to take a leadership role if things are going badly. In fact, the reluctance of executives to voice dissatisfaction with proceedings and to suggest alternative procedures is one very important reason why meetings so often fail to achieve their goals. If dissatisfaction with lack of progress is voiced, and is supported by other participants, then it is possible for the meeting to take a new direction and perhaps become more productive.

Fortunately most of the actions necessary to create successful meetings are very straightforward. Taking these steps does not absolutely guarantee that meetings will produce useful results, but if they are not taken a successful outcome is most unlikely.

THE IMPORTANCE OF TIME

In conducting successful meetings, time is a key element. Meetings should **begin promptly** at the time designated. Simple? Yet, how often do we attend meetings at which we sit around waiting to begin while the chairperson says something like: 'Let's wait a few moments more. Charlie and Ben said they were coming. Probably they have been held up.' The few minutes stretch until finally proceedings begin fifteen or twenty minutes later. It is instructive to contemplate what effect such behaviour has, assuming other participants allow the chairperson to act in this way.

What the chairperson is doing is to encourage latecoming. Participants in the meeting are likely to say: 'I'm not going to arrive on time and sit around twiddling my thumbs while I wait for others to turn up. I'll get there as late as I can. They can wait for me.' This attitude, which is quite realistic under the circumstances, virtually ensures that no meeting run by that chairperson will ever begin at the time stated.

However, should someone bring up the issue of starting on time as an agenda item, and it receives support from others, the chairperson can be forced to begin promptly. When everyone realizes the meeting will commence at a set time whether they are there or not, behaviour tends to change so that a full complement is likely to be present, ready to begin at the designated time. The resultant businesslike atmosphere thus created is conducive to effective decision making. Such an atmosphere is in marked contrast to the sloppiness of the casual: 'Let's wait for Charlie' alternative.

Finishing on time is important too. Most of us, especially if we are involved in business, need to schedule our working day. If we are uncertain when a meeting will conclude, it will be difficult for us to plan later activities. Again, an unbusinesslike atmosphere is created when such uncertainty is present. If agenda items are allowed to drag on endlessly, particularly early in the meeting then even though proceedings accelerate as the scheduled finishing time approaches, it is often impossible to cover everything. As a result the meeting is extended.

There are a number of ways in which this situation might be improved. The chairperson needs to exhibit firmness in bringing the meeting to a close at the designated time, perhaps indicating that items not discussed are to be postponed to a later date. Still, postponement of items is not a very satisfactory solution, so something more than finishing on time is necessary.

Usually, it is possible to **set a time limit on each agenda item**, thus ensuring that no one item is discussed for a time disporportionate to its perceived value. Though this procedure can improve meetings considerably, it is inevitable that it will not work perfectly. At times, quite unexpected issues of importance will surface, and these may demand quite lengthy discussion. However, because perfection is unobtainable in human affairs, that is not a reason for neglecting techniques, such as time-limited agendas, which work well most of the time.

Actually, this human atttribute of throwing the baby out with the bathwater when something does not work perfectly on all occasions is another of the Inner Game obstacles we need to overcome. I know of so many people, for example, who may be losing weight steadily, either through dieting or subconscious mental reprogramming, and who then have a bad day. Perhaps a dinner party has been their downfall, or maybe Christmas has proven too great a temptation. Having overeaten, they throw up their hands, saying 'What's the use', and go back to their previous pattern of overeating. A much more helpful attitude would be reflected in saying 'Well, that was a bad day, but I've got a fresh start coming up tomorrow'.

The same attitude may be adopted towards ideas like the time-limited agenda. Perhaps the technique did not achieve its purpose in a particular meeting because of some unusual set of circumstances. Still, there is a new meeting coming up next week, and the week after that. It will probably work well in those.

A final point on time. If, despite ending promptly and putting limits on each agenda item, meetings still do not seem to be accomplishing much, primarily because of long-winded discussion, reschedule starting times. For example, **begin at 11.30 a.m. or 4.30 p.m.** It is a truly wondrous thing to observe how great a sense of urgency permeates meetings when they are held before lunch or towards the end of the working day.

Participants watch the clock, speeding up proceedings so as not to be late for lunch or for getting home. Through this simple ploy, a monthly academic meeting in which I farticipated was reduced from an average time span of four-and-a-half hours to one-and-a-half hours. No deterioration in the quality of the decisions made was noticeable; in fact most of the academics taking part felt they were producing better results from the shorter meeting. All that was lost was the 'talking for the sake of talking' so beloved by many amongst us.

What appears to happen is that participants stick to the agenda, a vital ingredient of a successful meeting. When a chairperson permits wide ranging 'chatting' which is not really related to the specific item under consideration, he or she is undermining the effectiveness of the group through creation of a sense of frustration among the more businesslike attendees. Where someone wanders off the track, it is easy enough for the chairperson, or another participant, to ask: 'How is that relevant to X (the particular agenda item under discussion)?' If the person is able to demonstrate the relevance, well and good. If not, the meeting can then get back on the track and stop wasting time.

MORE TECHNIQUES FOR MAKING MEETINGS WORK

Even when attention is focused on specific agenda items without unnecessary sidetracking, time can be wasted by the way these items are introduced. Often the person presenting the point may speak at some length, 'waffling' on, perhaps repeating material already presented in the meeting papers, or talking in vague, general terms. To overcome this tendency, ask presenters to **provide a single page outline**. On it will appear:

1 the problem to be considered, defined in precise terms;
2 a number of alternative solutions;
3 the solution which the presenter thinks is 'best' together with several briefly expressed reasons for this choice.

All agenda items cannot be treated thus. Many can. The ones presented in this way usually generate discussion which is very goal oriented, and which result in precise decisions.

As a consultant, I often 'sit in' on meetings to observe the actual process which is taking place. Being largely ignorant of the meeting content, I am able to concentrate on what is actually going on. Increasingly, I have become aware of how few participants do their homework. By this I mean that they rarely read meeting papers beforehand, so they arrive without having given any thought to how they might present agenda items effectively. The brief, three step technique I have just described overcomes both these deficiencies. A one page summary of this nature takes little time to read in the actual meeting itself, and it immediately focuses discussion on the key issues.

Another feature present in successful meetings, but lacking in those ending in a sense of frustration, is frequent **summarizing**. It is helpful for either the chairperson or another participant to sum up, to draw together the threads of the discussion, to establish the point reached. At this time the goals of the meeting can be repeated and the contribution of the discussion towards the achievement of these assessed. Such checking helps to keep people 'on track', directing their energies towards attaining objectives seen as important.

Summarizing and objectives go hand in hand. People attending meetings need to know where they are heading, what they are trying to achieve. This means that **goals must be stated clearly at the outset**, and their importance agreed upon. Perhaps, sub-goals might be established and, as each is attained, a brief summary used to mark this stage in proceedings. Without the sense of direction engendered by the establishment of clear-cut objectives and the periodic review of progress in summary form, meetings often seem pointlessness.

Poor **minutes** will also contribute to this sense of futility which can so easily pervade meetings. Discursive, overfull minutes are often self-defeating, for their purpose is really to provide a brief, clear statement of proceedings which enhances the participants' feeling that they are achieving something and not wasting their time. If minutes are to achieve this purpose they need to include four elements.

- a record of decisions made;
- a statement of action which needs to be taken;
- a note of deadlines indicating when this action should be completed.
- identification of the person or persons who are to take responsibility for the necessary action.

Unless minutes embody this type of precise information, actions are not taken, or are postponed for too long. When responsibility is assigned, it is more difficult for excuses to be made. This is particularly so when clear deadlines are set.

When the minutes are read at the next meeting, normally as the first item of business, follow-up action is vitally important. If tasks are assigned as the result of one meeting, and progress on these tasks is not discussed at the next, people are encouraged to let things slip. Should deadlines not be enforced and people not be held responsible for taking action to meet those deadlines, they will find it relatively easy to adopt an attitude of: 'I'll get around to it'.

Such procrastination is not conducive to the successful conduct of a business in general or a meeting in particular. Therefore, it is likely to be helpful if we have some way of finding out whether the meetings conducted by our own firm can be labelled in this way.

THE EVALUATION OF MEETINGS

Many years ago, a writer whose name has been lost in the mists of time wrote these words: 'If you want to know the true value of a physician's work, do not ask the physician, ask his patient'. Aristotle, the Greek philosopher, made the same point when he affirmed that it is the guests at a dinner party who are in a better position to judge the merits of the meal than is the cook who prepared it. To find out, then, how successful a meeting has been, ask the people who attended it.

However, asking only one or two people at random is a risky business. This is particularly true of academic assessment. I was approached, on one occasion, by a very distraught university lecturer who wanted advice on how he could improve his teaching. Apparently his students thought his performance was terrrible. Four of them had come to see him, complaining about his methods. However, when I conducted an evaluation of his course, to which all the 157 students taking it contributed, I found that there were only four students who felt unhappy about it. The others were either neutral or positive.

George O'Neill, mentioned earlier in this book as a skilled negotiator, has shown himself to be aware of this problem by periodically checking on the meetings he conducts by asking *all* participants to answer a short questionnaire. To provide the opportunity for his executives to fill in the form, George finishes that particular meeting quarter-of-an-hour early.

The purpose of the exercise is to give George an idea of how effective the meeting was, and to permit the collection of information likely to lead to improvement on future occasions. Questionnaires can, if desired, be anonymous, for it is generally not necessary to find out which individual participants liked or disliked the meeting.

The form of questionnaire that George uses to gain the information needed to evaluate and improve upon meetings is that given on page 182.

This brief form many be used whenever occasion demands. If meetings have been going badly, perhaps it could be employed on three or four occasions in succession until things improve. Under other circumstances, it might be used every few weeks to check on the feelings of participants. It is such a simple idea, taking little time, yet

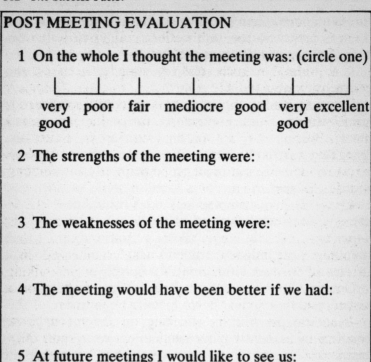

it produces benefits to a firm out of all proportion to the effort involved. This is true of many techniques, including those which apply to using yourself more effectively in meetings.

HOW TO EXERT INFLUENCE IN MEETINGS

You can exert your influence in meetings both non-verbally and verbally. Non-verbal influence has much to do with where you sit and how you sit. If you want to become more influential, seek a seat to the left-hand side of the chairperson, as close to him or her as possible, and facing in the same direction. Because people are conditioned to look towards the chairperson for guidance and control, you will be in a strong position to have your words listened to when you are seated in this way. Surprisingly enough, being seated on the chairperson's right hand is not as effective, although it is still better than sitting further away down the side of the table.

It is preferable to sit relatively quietly, speaking only when you have a definite contribution to make. Studies of influential people indicate that they say little compared to more verbose types, yet they are listened to more attentively. Because they are sparing with their words, waiting until they have something of value to say, their utterances exert an influence out of all propoprtion to the number of words spoken.

Conversely, people who talk a lot often have little influence, even when what they say may be insightful and important. Like the boy who cried 'wolf' too often, their valuable contributions become lost, submerged in a stream of verbiage. When such a person begins talking, others tend to think: 'Oh, there goes Don, waffling on as usual', and they simply 'turn off' until he finishes.

In addition to speaking sparingly, it is helpful for you to use a signal to indicate your readiness to contribute. Clicking a pen usually works well, the sound attracting the attention of other participants. Clearing the throat is not as good for this purpose as it is a sound heard so often at meetings that it has lost much of its signalling power. However, changing your position in the seat still serves as an effective indication that you are ready to speak. If you normally sit upright or lean back, move forward towards the table. This could be accompanied by a movement of your feet on the floor to serve as an attention-gaining sound.

Once you have signified your intention to speak through such non-verbal cues, it is necessary to exert your influence with words. Be brief, presenting your ideas in short sentences with dramatic pauses. Avoid negatives. Instead, use positive, affirmative sentences, spoken in a quiet voice with occasional loudness for emphasis. People who constantly speak loudly have an adverse effect on their listeners, particularly if, as is so often the case, they are also verbose. On most occasions, the quiet, firm voice commands attention. The loud one does not.

When you speak, attempt to use things others have said. A point which has been made in several different contexts in this book involves helping other people to feel important. If you can make another person feel valued and worthy, you have gone a long way towards winning a friend for life, someone who will support you and be influenced by what you say. So, wherever possible, repeat the last thing said, make a positive comment about the person who uttered it, then use it to develop your own idea, saying something like: 'Bob, you really expressed that idea well. I'd like to build on it by. . . .'

Referring to people by name and acknowledging their ideas is a most successful way of exerting influence, not only in meetings but in life generally. This is true, in fact, for virtually all the points I have attempted to make in this book. The things that work well in helping you to be more successful in business are also likely to help you be more successful in your life generally.

Success, as we have seen, can mean different things to different people. Only you can decide what it means to you. Through using the various approaches described in this book you will be better able to see what is important to you and the most effective ways of arriving at where you want to be. Self-awareness, self-discipline, self-motivation, and self-direction all play their parts, meshing into a system which will, I hope, enable you to experience all the success you desire and, as a result, greatly enhance your enjoyment of life.

Bibliography

Brown, H. *How I Found Freedom in an Unfree World*. New York: Mac-Millan, 1973.

Cohen, H. *You Can Negotiate Anything*. Secaucus, N.J.: Lyle Stuart, 1980.

Drucker, P. *The Efficient Executive*. New York: Harper & Row, 1966.

Ellis, A., & Harper, R. A. *A New Guide to Rational Living*. Hollywood, Calif.: Wilshire, 1975.

Frankl, V. *Man's Search for Meaning*. New York: Basic Books, 1963.

Gallwey, W. T. *The Inner Game of Tennis*. New York: Random House, 1974.

Hopkins, T. *How to Master the Art of Selling*. Scottsdale, Arizona: Chamion Press, 1980.

Houston, J. *The Possible Human*. Los Angeles: J. P. Tarcher, 1982.

Korda, M. *Success*. New York: Random House, 1977.

Kriegel, R., & Kriegel, M. H. *The C Zone : Peak Performance Under Pressure*. New York: Doubleday, 1984.

Leopold, R. *The Quest for Excellence*. Melbourne: Business Education Institute, 1981.

Lodge, D. *Ginger, You're Barmy*. London: Secker & Warburg, 1962.

McMaster, M., & Grinder, J. *Precision*. Beverly Hill, Calif.: Precision Models, 1980.

Moine, D. J., & Herd, J. H. *Modern Persuasion Strategies*. Englewood Cliffs, N.J.: Prentice-Hall, 1984.

Silva, J. *The Silva Mind Control Method for Business Managers*. Englewood Cliffs, N.J.: Prentice-Hall, 1983.

Stanton, H. E. *The Plus Factor*. Sydney: Fontana/Collins, 1979.

Stanton, H. E. *The Healing Factor*. Sydney: Fontana/Collins, 1981.

Stanton, H. E. *The Stress Factor*. Sydney: Fontana/Collins, 1983.

Stanton, H. E. *The Fantasy Factor*. Sydney: Fontana/Collins, 1985.

INDEX

About the Author

After graduating from Melbourne University, Dr Stanton spent eight years teaching in secondary schools and five years lecturing in teacher training colleges. He has taught in the universities of South Australia and Tasmania since 1969, and is now Consultant on Higher Education at the University of Tasmania. He also runs a consultancy service for companies and the public sector, and has a private practice in clinical and sports psychology.

Dr Stanton is author of the following books, also published by Optima:

The Plus Factor: A Guide to Positive Living
ISBN 0-356-15195-6
The Healing Factor: A Guide to Positive Health
ISBN 0-356-15194-8
The Stress Factor: A Guide to More Relaxed Living
ISBN 0-356-15192-1
The Fantasy Factor: Using Your Imagination to Solve Everyday Problems
ISBN 0-356-15193-X